About the Author

Wilena G. Brown is a United Church minister whose years of experience and academic study have led to reflection on the inter-relationships of, and reasons for, the varied understandings and practices of the Christian faith. A native of Nova Scotia, Wilena received her Master of Divinity degree from Emmanuel College in Toronto, followed by a Master's degree in Pastoral Theology from Princeton Theological Seminary. She began her ministry in Consort, Alberta, in 1953, and moved to Edmonton in 1957. She then served at Forest Hill United Church in Toronto and at the General Council offices of the United Church. In 1975, Wilena moved to Western Ontario, where she served at the Bluevale-Whitechurch, Varna-Goshen, and Millbank-Hampstead pastoral charges. She served for many years as a senator of Victoria University and as a member of the Emmanuel College Council. Wilena has had numerous articles published in both journals and magazines. She now resides in Dundas, Ontario.

Faithstyles
in
Congregations

*Living Together
in a Christian
Community*

Faithstyles
in
Congregations

*Living Together
in a Christian
Community*

Wilena G. Brown

THE UNITED CHURCH PUBLISHING HOUSE

Every effort has been made to contact the owners of copyrighted material reprinted herein. The publisher will be pleased to include further acknowledgements in future editions of this book. Grateful acknowledgement is made for permission to reprint from the following:

From *The Different Drum* by M. Scott Peck. Copyright © 1987 by M. Scott Peck, M.D., P.C. Reprinted by permission of Simon & Schuster, Inc.;

Unique Dynamics of the Small Church by Carl. S. Dudley. Copyright © 1977 The Alban Institute, Inc., 4550 Montgomery Avenue, Suite 433N, Bethseda, MD 20814. All rights reserved. Reprinted with permission;

Faith Development and Pastoral Care by James Fowler, copyright © 1987 Fortress Press. Used by permission of Augsburg Fortress;

Land and Community by Alex Sim. Copyright © 1988 by Alex Sim. Used by permission;

Psalms Now by Leslie F. Brandt. Copyright © 1973 Concordia Publishing House. Used with permission;

The Spirit and Forms of Love by Daniel Day Williams. Copyright © 1968 by HarperCollins Publishers. Used by permission;

In Search of Wisdom by Verna Ross McGiffin. Copyright © 1990 by Verna Ross McGiffin. Used by permission of Wood Lake Books;

Continued on page 180.

Canadian Cataloguing in Publication Data

Brown, Wilena G. (Wilena Grace), 1929-
        Faithstyles in congregations : living together in
a Christian community

Includes bibliographical references and index.
ISBN 1-55134-006-2

1. Faith - Psychology. 2. Pastoral psychology.
3. Spiritual formation. I. Title.

BT771.2.B76 1994   253.5'3   C94-930748-3

The United Church Publishing House
85 St. Clair Avenue East
Toronto, Ontario
M4T 1M8

Publisher: R.L. Naylor
Editor-in-Chief: Peter Gordon White
Managing Editor: Elizabeth Phinney
Book Design: Chris Dumas, Dept. of Graphics and Print
Printed in Canada by: Kromar Printing Ltd.

5 4 3 2 1 94 95 96 97 98

*To all who who have shared
their yearnings,
struggles, and joys
with me,
as faith grew in their lives.*

Contents

Foreword

Wilena Brown writes from the perspective of one who knows she is a partner—a partner with God, a partner with the whole faith community, indeed, a partner with all of creation. She presents an intriguing analysis of congregational life in a down-to-earth fashion that resonates with the wisdom garnered from her years of experience in living, and specifically in living out, a pastoral ministry. Here is a work that, in my opinion, would well serve rural faith communities willing to examine who they are and to ask questions about where they are going. However, it is also a book that could help the most urban of congregations with their task of naming the nature of their community and the focus of their mission.

The author invites us to consider three main groupings for the persons who constitute a congregation. These are described as faithstyles: the community faithstyle, the searcher faithstyle, and the partnership faithstyle. By moving us through a consideration of each group's response to various doctrines or teachings of the church, Brown gives us the opportunity to consider how communications may flounder and projects and plans become jeopardized as persons from the different faith stances misinterpret and misjudge one another. We are encouraged to understand the fears and angers or frustrations that may characterize each group. Likewise, we glimpse the hopes and aspirations each may know. Understanding the different faith stances gives us another base for appreciating how programmes may be perceived as threatening by some and promising by others.

Faithstyles in Congregations should serve as a useful tool to persons in paid, accountable ministries, who need not only understand for themselves what happens in congregation but who must be able to interpret some of this within the congregation, its organizations, and boards. Such understanding may help us avoid the destructive patterns of blame and counter-blame, accusation and counter-accusation, that too often sap congregational strength and sabotage programmes and outreach ministries.

Other areas of exploration could augment the useful considerations the author outlines for us. These might include a consideration of the factors that cause us to be found in different faithstyle groupings at different times in our lives: how our individual personality types and our compulsions make us more prone to move to one or another of the groupings; and how those in leadership also manifest, at different times, characteristics belonging to one or another of the faithstyles and the impact this has on congregational life. Personally, I would want to look at how each grouping tends to deal with grief—for we are, many of us, active grievers and many of our communities are in deep traumatic grieving *as communities*. It would be useful to explore how cynicism is played out for each grouping. It may cause searchers or partnership groups to take on the characteristics of a community faithstyle without ever knowing what has happened.

Congregations and those in paid, accountable ministry have been given a tool, a very usable tool with which to examine and interpret congregational life in order to nurture and plan for renewal and purposeful ministries. In addition to drawing upon her experience and a deep commitment to people, Brown draws on the wisdom of a wide variety of scholars from different disciplines whose work has encouraged and enabled her own ministry. While I was Moderator of The United Church of Canada, my visits took me into many very different situations where people were reassessing their place as a faith community within the wider community. They looked for a tool or resource to address their situation. Here is one that awaits our enthusiastic and imaginative use. Who knows in what exciting directions we may be led by the Spirit of God working in and with us? Openness to that, and openness for that, is part of what *Faithstyles in Congregations* calls us towards.

The Very Rev. Dr. Walter H. Farquharson
Saltcoats, Saskatchewan

Acknowledgements

So many people have been involved in this book, and over so many years, that it is hard indeed to choose who to thank. I want immediately to acknowledge the trust and support of three remarkable people: Dr. James Muir, Mrs. Jean Muir, and Mrs. Stephanie Stewart. They had confidence in me and, at very different times in my life, created opportunities for me that I would not otherwise have had. I wish they were alive to see this finished work.

I am grateful to my family, to the teachers in the one-room school where I learned how exciting reading can be, and to the teachers of Colchester County Academy in Truro. It was at a debate that Dr. Mosher first got me interested in public speaking. Dr. Jim Endicott, on a Crusade, inspired me to think of ministry when I was only fifteen and female ministers were scarce. I also thank my professors at Victoria and Emmanuel in Toronto, and at Princeton Theological Seminary.

I thank the pastoral charges that helped me to grow in understanding: Consort in Alberta, Robertson in Edmonton, Forest Hill in Toronto, and Bluevale-Whitechurch, Varna-Goshen, and Millbank-Hampstead—all in south-western Ontario. I was at Varna-Goshen for seven years and that is where the ideas which underlie this book began to come together. I thank all of the people who shared with me some of their deepest thoughts and feelings about God and life. This includes a large number of people who attended group sessions and courses through the years.

I have been able to work the last sixteen years due to Dr. K. W. G. Brown, who dared to experiment with a new heart drug when I had a long period of severe cardiac limitations. The experience of being back in the pastorate gave me such joy that I referred to the change as a resurrection.

The Ventures in Mission programme of the United Church gave me a five-year financial grant that allowed me to work on a project entitled "Re-development of Rural Ministry." I thank Harry Ousseron and the Division of Ministry Personnel and Education for this help. I thank, too, the people who formed my network across Canada and the United States. I had a lot of input from the experts—the people actually working with congregations. I also thank the Division of Mission in Canada, which invested in the developmental costs of this book. Andra Owen and Richard Chambers were an enormous help to me while the work proceeded.

There are many others: co-leaders of the Southern Ontario Orientation to Rural Ministry programme, Neil Lackey, Richard Hollingsworth, and John King, all of whom worked with me to help ordinands and commissionands adjust to the realities of their new situations; Alex Sim, a wonderful source of wisdom and encouragement; Sharon Wilson Menzies, Douglas and Elizabeth Chapman, Robert Thaler, Pat Krug and Joan Berge, all of whom made valuable suggestions, at different times, about the text; Marvin Anderson, who worked on editing the manuscript until other commitments intervened; Elizabeth Phinney, for her skill and painstaking care in preparing the manuscript for publication; and Walter Farquharson, for writing the foreword.

The work, of course, as it stands, is my interpretation of the realities. It is intended to stimulate thought and experimentation towards new models of how to live together in congregations, in healthier and more enjoyable ways. I take full responsibility for it.

Introduction

This book was written, after considerable study and reflection on a wide range of theories and practices, for those who wish to understand more of the possibilities inherent in the Christian faith. It presents a model for using insights of faith development theory and spirituality in the actual life of congregations. I hope to show that the central work of ministry is aided by an understanding of, and willingness to work with, different styles of faith. These can be delineated and understood as normal and productive in a Christian life. I have called the three styles "community," "searching," and "partnership," and it is in this order that the views of each faithstyle are explored in the second part of this book.

Such an approach to ministry accomplishes at least three helpful things. First, it affirms the faith already present in the people of a congregation. Second, it opens the door to growth and change without fear, judgement, or isolation. Third, it tends to unify congregations as respect for a variety of faithstyles grows.

A major area of difference between general faith development principles and those I have developed revolves around "stages" of development. Changes are usually seen as progressive, and occurring in a predictable pattern. Such writers as James W. Fowler, John H. Westerhoff III, and M. Scott Peck (to whom I am indebted) believe that the work of one stage has to be completed before one can move on to another.

James W. Fowler's *Stages of Faith: The Psychology of Human Development and the Quest for Meaning* was "a trail-blazing" book for me. Fowler delineates six stages: Intuitive-Projective; Mythic-Literal; Synthetic-Conventional; Individuative-Reflective; Conjunctive; and Universalizing.[1] During a conversation with him, he recommended to me that a simpler form might be used for the purpose of general Christian education.

John H. Westerhoff III has developed valuable models for congregational use. In *Liturgy and Learning through the Life Cycle*, co-authored by William H. Willimon, three stages are used: Affiliative; Searching; and Integrated.[2] These have formed the basis of my thinking.

M. Scott Peck is a psychiatrist whose best-selling books *The Road Less Traveled* and *The Different Drum* deal with the inter-relationships of psychology and faith. He presents four stages of spiritual growth: Chaotic, antisocial; Formal, institutional; Skeptic, individual; and Mystic, communal.[3]

There are undoubtedly other representative views of faith development. I have chosen to use Westerhoff and Willimon's typology, but I omit the concept of stages as they presented them. I use the word "faithstyles" to emphasize, first of all, that people do not progress through stages in an ever predictable way and, second, that congregations have people gifted in constantly changing and different ways. I therefore take the position that the presence of all three faithstyles needs to be constantly recognized and affirmed in every congregation. To my knowledge, this may be the first attempt to offer a general interpretation of the place of faithstyles in the practice of pastoral ministry. Others have dealt more specifically with the relationship of faithstyles to Christian education and preaching.

This work began with reflection on the community faithstyle as it is experienced in small rural churches. My United Church of Canada Ventures in Mission grant was specifically targeted for "Re-Development of Rural Ministry." Before considering how to re-develop, I needed to explore the present realities at a deeper level. This effort revealed that while what I now call the community faithstyle was dominant, it was not the only faithstyle within any congregation. It is, however, immensely powerful in many congregations and may inhibit either the development or expression of other styles. Pastors who responded to my 1987 questionnaire indicated that this was a common frustration—

particularly if they were recent graduates of theological schools.

While I was pursuing this study, The United Church of Canada was rocked by the question of possible ordination of homosexuals. The lid blew off of conventional theological assumptions, which had been held for generations. Emotions ran high. The need to examine whether God's will might be in conflict with what had been simply accepted as right by those with a community faithstyle created great stress. Large numbers of people were shaken enough to want to understand more fully what the issues really were. Bible study groups flourished. I learned an important lesson about my subject—there was a lot of growth in people's ability to experience and name their own faith in public. In faith development terms, the issue was a catalyst, moving many community faithstyle persons into a searching style, at least briefly. People wanted to know *why* and *how* different positions could be held. They wanted to make up their own minds.

During the examination of this issue, I became more conscious of the role of the third faithstyle, which I call the partnership style. Partners with God, as I define them, tended to raise the religious faith questions about the matter. For example, at one meeting where a homophobic was holding forth strongly, a partner quietly asked, "What do you think Jesus would say about this?" The tone of the meeting changed radically.

In the actual experiences of a congregation it is helpful to have people who speak from different faith perspectives. How the leader responds, however, is crucial to the outcome. Many leaders are not able to tolerate, let alone encourage, divergent views. Therefore, I have concluded that pastoral leaders need to be trained in the facilitation of groups, so that growth in faith may take place through activities such as business meetings, as well as adult study groups. In these ways a congregation may become more authentically the Body of Christ in its local community.

It is important to note what different faithstyles take to be their source of authority. For the community faithstyle, the authority lies in their community of faith: its traditions, its shared experiences, its formal faith statements and accepted practices. The individual is expected to conform to community standards. For the searching faithstyle, the source of authority is in one's own mind and what one believes to be the truth. Searchers may sometimes condemn institutions as destructive. They tend to question everything. This may be hard for a local church congregation to accept. Authority for the partnership style rests in God and Self, or, if you prefer, Self and God. One's whole being, including one's mind and its conclusions, are brought into a living, dynamic relationship with God. Both the traditions of the community faithstyle and the questing of searchers are accepted. Partners emphasize time with God and seek to find God's leadership and companionship for their lives.

In today's mainline churches, the battle lines are often clearly drawn between community faithstyle persons and searchers. Many faithful church members live with the fear that the historic faith they have treasured will be destroyed. I try to show that this fear can be considerably lessened if the importance of searching is understood. Searchers work at consciously making their received tradition their own. In contemporary society, the importance of one's self is perhaps over-emphasized, and yet the search for self-assurance is fundamental to one's identity. We all need to be affirmed and supported in our quest.

It would be enormously helpful if people could learn to communicate better regarding the different styles. Peck says that community faithstyle persons are "very threatened by the individualists and skeptics of Stage III [the searching style], and even more by the mystics of Stage IV [the partnership style], who seem to believe in the same sorts of things they do, but believe in them with a freedom they find absolutely terrifying." Searchers "are cowed by Stage IV people [partners], who seem to be scientific-minded like themselves ... yet somehow still believe in this crazy God business."[4] The feeling of threat between the different faithstyles needs to be taken very seriously.

To be the Body of Christ in today's world is extremely difficult. This book is intended to provide help for the large number of people in congregations who feel confused about the role of the Christian faith today. It shows that there are many ways of experiencing faith. A community that celebrates that fact, instead of finding it a problem, is able to assist people in developing a faith that meets their needs. Those who are thus satisfied will find ways to share their faith in the world about them. I hope that this book will provoke discussion and new practices to comfortably hold those who are ready for new ways of relating to one another and to God.

To help clarify what I mean by faithstyles, let me tell you about Susan and her family.

Susan was angry. She had told her parents that she planned to spend a weekend with her friends at a cottage. Her parents said "No!", and stuck with it despite her many days of pleading. She had exhausted the "Don't you trust me?" and the "Everyone else is going!" arguments, to no avail. Her parents, to her exasperation, always came back to "What would people think?" To Susan it was not an acceptable reason to refuse her request. To her parents it was the most important one of all.

Susan's parents are part of a complex reality that I call the community faithstyle. All of their lives are governed by their faith community's standards. To them, what felt right, and what would be judged right by the community, *was* right.

Occasionally Susan realized that her parents had a comfortable acceptance of limits that she did not share. She was busy exploring, making her own decisions, building a different way of life. I call this the searcher faithstyle. It was not always easy for Susan, especially when she was at home in the familiar community. She had learned to be quiet—not to raise the thorny question, not to argue when outrageous things were said to her. She felt like less of a person then, and often wondered if her parents had ever recognized the traditional community pressures on them.

Susan sometimes went to visit her neighbour, whom she called Nana, when things became too hard or confusing. Nana was over eighty, and both her vision and her hearing were failing. Arthritis made it hard for her to walk. But Nana was at peace. She understood both Susan and Susan's parents very well. Nana had followed her own family's community faithstyle until she was over thirty. As a young mother with an undependable husband, Nana had begun to question why she should suffer, why she couldn't go to work and earn money to feed and clothe her children, why her vow to be faithful "till death do us part" should mean endless pain for her.

Nana had dared to go against her faith community and her family and had managed to build a new place for herself. She had not lost her religious faith. Instead, when the period of adjustment was over, she was seen by all to have a strong, deep, and meaningful faith, a faith quite different from that of her early years or her later years of struggle. She had brought her questions to bear on her inherited faith and was gradually able to see both good and bad in the old and the new ways. She came to understand that God was in all ways. Her life became a partnership with God. I call this the partnership faithstyle. Susan longed for this faithstyle but could not understand that she was actually moving towards it. It seemed to her to be a special gift Nana had been given.

These three faithstyles, and variations of them, co-exist in most of our churches. In some, one faithstyle dominates, in others, another. In a few churches, they are balanced. I estimate that the community faithstyle forms a majority in Canadian churches. I believe, however, that we have a higher number of silent searchers in our congregations than we are aware of—

perhaps as high as 30 per cent. I also believe that we have more partnership people than we know because many of the people who live it do not feel comfortable talking about it. In some cases, they may not know what words are commonly used to describe their experiences and fear being considered strange or even crazy. It is important for them to establish contact with others on a similar faith path so that they can feel confident that this is an acceptable faithstyle even if different from the "normal" one in their community. A reasonable estimate of their number in a typical congregation may be 10 to 15 per cent. Their number is growing, but many do not remain in mainline churches.

Primarily, this data means that no matter how homogeneous a congregation may appear to be, it is seldom homogeneous on the faith level. People may agree to live by certain rules in their faith community, and practice traditional forms of worship, but they look at things in different ways. They ask different questions, though perhaps never aloud. They have a variety of religious experiences. They relate to their faith community in everything from a begrudging to a contented way. And all this changes from time to time, as people move through the "seasons of adulthood"—from choices about a partner, family, or career responsibilities to empty nest and retirement issues. Faith is also affected by health and economic concerns.

We relate to communities— either secular or faith—according to our situation and our needs at different times. There is, in reality, no solid block of truth to which anyone relates, in the same way, through all of life. Congregations, like families, have histories and present realities and hopes for the future. They may shape us but we also shape them. How this interaction happens is what this book is about.

Wilena G. Brown
Dundas, Ontario
March 1994

I

THE FAITHSTYLES

Chapter One

The Community Faithstyle

Faith is the substance of things hoped for, the evidence of things not seen.

Hebrews 11:1, *KJV*

A family moving into a new community looks for clues as to its nature. They will usually check out facilities they may need—schools, hospitals, swimming pools, day care, sports arenas. In reviewing the local churches, the Sunday church school, the choir, the women's group, the emphasis on social action, all may be evaluated. The pastor's style of preaching and the warmth or chill of the welcome extended may be most important. The not-so-obvious qualities that make the community either joyful or painful are harder to grasp. However, first impressions are not always dependable. As one lives in a community, layer after layer of reality is revealed.

There are so many things to discover in a community or church that it helps if one loves a mystery. As one attends events and talks to people, clues to the way things work in this particular place gradually emerge. I have found through experience that there are some general principles that lay a trail worth following. I call them "laws of community interaction," because I have

3

never found them absent in any small community. Carl S. Dudley, author of *Unique Dynamics of the Small Church*, says that congregations of fewer than one hundred members and in which everyone knows everyone else constitute a primary group, like a family. Naturally the members affect each other's lives.[1] Large churches tend to have a number of small groups centred on special interests, such as the physical building, Christian education, social action, Bible study, or prayer.

The first law of community interaction is: *There is always a reason for any action or reaction.* It may not be a reason that makes sense to an outsider, but it has been shaped by experience in the community (which is, of course, what the outsider lacks). The smaller the community, the more individual the reason may be. For example, a leading person of a congregation may have a prejudice against change of any kind. It may take many months and the combined efforts of everyone else in the congregation to finally convince such a person that the choir *could* sit in a different place at the front of the sanctuary. The outsider may conclude that "they won't change anything here" while the process goes on, but then be startled when it is announced at a board meeting that "it's okay now." Sometimes such things are explained, sometimes they are not.

The second law of community interaction is: *Decision making is a complicated matter when feelings are involved.* For community faithstyle persons, feelings are always involved. In fact, the group may not even be conscious of the feelings that drive it. For example, a community or church group may wish to establish a day care programme. A survey may prove the need, suitable leadership may be available, funds may not be a problem, yet resistance may be very high. One factor may be that a number of important persons believe that, in the natural order of things, parents should look after their own children. Unconsciously, they may identify with the children in feeling neglected by their parents. When outsiders first meet resistance that they do not understand, it is wise for them to consider such resistance in light of unconscious influences.

Some of the obvious warning signs of emotional involvement might include the fact that normal business meeting procedures are not followed. In many cases, ideas are discussed before a motion is made or seconded. When a consensus is reached, or the attitudes of all made clear, a person may make a motion "for the books," or they may just agree. Another warning sign may be that things are weighed on a personal level rather than on their merit. If Tom is against something and Stella is for it, the group may feel that it has to take sides—not on the issue, but on which relationship is most important to them. A chairperson may be frustrated by silence. Negotiation may be timidly begun. Or someone may say, "We can't decide this without more people here," or some other statement that delays a decision. There may be an audible sigh of relief. Informal discussions will go on outside the meeting format and the next thing the chairperson may hear about it is that a decision has been reached. It may be announced at the next meeting—or it may not.

This leads us to the third law of community interaction: *Relationships are more important than issues.* In traditionally stable communities, an outsider may be puzzled to hear, "I can't vote for that because I live beside Kim, who is against it, and I have to get along with Kim for a whole lot of years." Ethical questions are, therefore, much more complicated and sometimes ignored because of the higher value placed on maintaining harmonious relationships.[2]

The fourth law of community interaction is: *There are a number of networks.* These networks process everything that happens or is said to have happened or that may happen. They may be based on kinship groups, on being neighbours or old school pals, on sharing similar tastes—almost anything. They are seldom obvious to outsiders, and there is no way of being sure of who belongs to any one network. Networks work in different ways. Some are primarily factual; some become increasingly fictional along the way. In order to deal with networks, one must know the difference between information innocently communicated and "stories" with evil intentions. The first is essential for the life of a caring community; the second brings death to relationships.

From the outside, a community faithstyle group looks and feels somewhat like a well-wound ball of yarn: when the top layer is removed, more complexity is revealed; pressure exerted at one point results in reactions all through the ball; and trying to dig out the middle ruins the whole thing. One has to be respectful of how it is put together and work with the exposed reality in a responsible way.

From the inside, a community faithstyle group may be either comfortable for an outsider or enormously frustrating. Four factors form a box within which the well-adapted move. I have named the sides of the box "social pressure," "guilt," "doctrines," and "traditions—the 'right way of doing things.'" It looks like this:

Community Faithstyle

Authority: Community

Key Words: What Will Others Think?

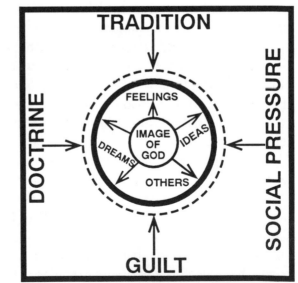

6

I am assuming the image of God in each person and suggest that the interaction between God's reality and the individual is limited by the "I shoulds" and the "I musts" of the persons brought up in this style. Many persons are conscious of both the internal and external pressure suggested here.

Social pressure can be a powerful and changing force. For example, in the 1950s, women wore hats and gloves to church. Men wore shirts and ties. Now, in some churches, almost anything is worn. There is still pressure, however, to be quiet in church and to obediently kneel, stand, read. In the same way, one is pressured by custom into rituals to mark life's major events, such as births, marriages, deaths. Gatherings, such as showers, are often held by the community for each of its members. What is done for one must be done for all. Everyone rallies around when someone loses a loved one—especially if the deceased is young. A great deal of caring is expressed by these actions and a clear statement is made: *we recognize that you are one of us.*

This recognition requires a responsibility of everyone in the group, which they or may not accept. If someone is burned out, everyone will do what they can to help. They know that if it happened to them, they too would be helped. Many communities are proud of their record in this regard, but it is unreasonable to suppose that this support is always given willingly. Part of the reason it is given is that a person may feel guilty if he or she doesn't do what is expected. Startling evidence of this is found in how some communities exclude "new people" from such reciprocity. Who you are is what counts, and whether or not you play by the same rules determines how others treat you. Of course, another factor is also at work—people really love to get together to do something worthwhile. Both men and women have roles to play in many of the community's undertakings. I remember well the work parties held to prepare a house for our coming refugee family. It was interesting for me to see men on their knees scrubbing floors—something they didn't often do at home, I was led to understand!

Guilt is an extremely persuasive tool in a community faithstyle group. The word refers to both the inward reaction of a person who acknowledges that he or she has done something wrong and to the outward attitude of the group that regards the action as a sin. An individual whose behaviour is extreme is reprimanded in the church by excommunication, being "shunned," or "sent to Coventry" (no longer talked with)—in other words by being cut off from the community itself. If one steps out of place, one is punished. Whether formal or informal ridicule is used, confrontation or disapproving looks, the message is clearly sent: "You have done wrong!" The action may have been a little thing, such as presuming to take a leadership role in a social action group; or a big thing, such as starting a petition to get rid of a professional person who is inadequate or destructive; or a personal, family thing, such as leaving a spouse. Whatever it is, if it is perceived as threatening to the life of the community, it is condemned. Laying on the guilt is the community's reaction to the fear of its faithstyle's destruction. It is *never* to be taken lightly!

A person has to be strong and determined to carry on with such a load. The guilt inside may be just a small, annoying voice of unease that says, "You're out of your proper place," or it may be a crushing burden that destroys a person's life. Whatever it is, it is hard, not only for the one involved, but for all of his or her relatives and friends. A vivid example of this was portrayed in the television movie *Evil in Clear River*. The heroine led a campaign against an allegedly anti-Semitic teacher and not only suffered the consequences herself but caused her husband and son rough times too. She was an "outsider," who had married into an old family of the area. As a result of her leadership in this issue, she was told clearly that she was no longer one of the community. Despite her struggles and the pain of her friends' desertion, she did not give in to pressure. This level of strength may not be possible for everyone to maintain.

Doctrine tells people what their beliefs should be. The controlling doctrines may be based on early Sunday school lessons or remembered Bible stories rather than on clearly thought out principles. Sometimes people are told that they must not question. The impression given is that God is a kind of magician, and we only have to believe what the Bible, our parent, or teacher or preacher say. The fact that a teaching makes no logical sense may be considered unimportant. This attitude is incredibly difficult for some people to handle and they drop out without knowing that there are other ways of looking at these faith statements.

One of the recurring problems concerns how the Bible is interpreted. If the community has taught its members that the Bible cannot be wrong in any way, a person who comes to a study of geology in school has a problem. If God created the universe in six days (around 4004 B.C., some Bibles used to note in the margin), how can scientists deal with millions of years of evidence? The fact that the Bible is more about meaning than about science may not be a part of the doctrine taught. The doctrine of a particular congregation may include some confusing, even contradictory "facts," which make a reasonable faith appear impossible. This may cause some to feel discouraged about trying to understand. They must either accept it all or reject it all—at least on the surface. Those who accept are welcomed happily into the faith community. Those who reject anything are often told that they are being prayed for and may even be punished by exclusion from the faith community.

Tradition, as accepted by a faith community, results in practices based on shared beliefs. The practice of saying grace before meals may be a grateful acknowledgement of food received, or a habit that, if missed, causes a guilty feeling. Going to church may bring strength to live through the week, or it may be a time to see and be seen, to hear the latest news. If one is to be a "good member," one must respect whatever forms the community faithstyle value system takes.

There is currently an enormous amount of guilt and pain

around the issue of church attendance. Younger people are often refusing to participate in the established practices. This may cause deep anger and distress in the community. The smaller the congregation, the more pressure is exerted on each member to carry his or her weight. Resentment may build and the faith community may be broken. The beliefs expressed in the old forms are often what make the community faithstyle what it is. Many persons cannot believe that it is possible to be Christian in any other way.

It is clear, then, that whether or not one is content in a community faithstyle depends on whether traditional limits feel good and right. If they do not, suffering will likely result. The struggle to find a different faith may be long and hard, and some never succeed. So there is a risk in stepping outside the box, but it is also true that there are risks in staying inside. A serious problem has appeared within families: Grandparents may demand faithfulness to a church in the old terms, and grandchildren may simply refuse to obey. Parents may be caught in a terrible struggle over the meaning of faith and faithfulness that spans all three generations.

A second serious problem for community faithstyle persons is coping with change. If one "has to believe" that God rewards good people, for example, why is it that we have drought, poor markets, losses, fears, and family tragedies? Why are our communities being destroyed by strange new persons coming in and trusted old ones moving out? Why have the standards of society sunk so low? Has the Devil taken control? Such changes are very hard for community faithstyle persons to understand and harder still for them to manage. It can lead them to despair. We will look further into this in the following chapters.

Furthermore, being inside a community faithstyle group frequently feels *safe* to those within it because everyone knows, more or less, what to expect from the others. It may not be all sweetness and light, but it is predictable. Many people dream great dreams but never take the first step towards realizing them, often fearing being seen as different, or "standing out." The comfort of recurring patterns may dull any adventurous urges. One unhappy community faithstyle person undoubtedly spoke for many when she reported that she found her faith community "smothering."

It is important to remember that people see themselves and each other *as they were* as well as how they are now. Sometimes that is a good and happy thing; sometimes it is tragic. The most outstanding memory for many people is that of their wedding day. Those who criticize the amount of time and money spent on weddings need to remember that it is a way of celebrating a time when everything seems possible and we are at our best. There are also memories of youthful "wildness," which are like shadows over some; or of an illness, such as depression or epilepsy, which, though now healed or controlled, still causes distrust in the present. If such afflicted persons move to a new community to make a new start, they lose their "place" in a somewhat predictable society.

It is interesting to talk with older persons whose memories include the lives of several generations. They can trace family characteristics, sometimes with a sense of fatalism, but they can also marvel at what some people were able to achieve despite problematic backgrounds. Even the unexpected beauty found in a drab garden, the wonder of natural life unfolding without anyone really understanding how or why, brings with it hope when least expected. It is possible to change the most predictable of patterns!

Questions to Consider

1. Do you agree with the so-called "laws of community interaction"? Do you know any that were missed?
2. Have you ever done something of which you are ashamed because you felt that you had to please some person or group?
3. Have you ever been shocked or angered by something you found out or realized about other church members?
4. In what ways do you think it helps to have community standards of faith and practice? Are there ways in which it can hurt?
5. Are you satisfied with your church as it is?

Chapter Two

The Searcher Faithstyle

There lives more faith in honest doubt,
Believe me, than in half the creeds.
Alfred, Lord Tennyson,
"In Memoriam," xcv

Searchers are often hidden from view. They tend to take on the protective colouring (language and behaviour) of the dominant community faithstyle in most small or rural churches. When the church is centred on the issue of survival, those who question or pursue a different goal are not really welcome. Some remain hidden in the congregation. Some set off fireworks with questions and/or objections and are seen as "difficult." Others simply leave if an alternative is available.

Searchers tend to dart around if someone tries to pin them down. But if they are offered "food" of the right sort, they gather fast and appreciatively. They feel welcome in a group that offers them both freedom *and* nourishment. The members of the Baby Boom generation are particularly inclined towards a searcher faithstyle, but there are no set limits with regard to age, education, church affiliation, or any other factor. If one talks at a deep enough level with almost any church member, some questions and disagreements with accepted beliefs will be found. For example, very few people in mainline churches appear to believe in a traditional heaven. They accept that people are with God, but the details are usually vague.

Those who intentionally become searchers are hungry for more knowledge and understanding. A sharp difference lies between searchers and community faithstyle persons, who have a more unconsciously absorbed faith. There are three common reasons for searchers to seek further understanding of the nature of their faith and practice: a change in one's life; a change in one's environment; an incompletely understood drive from within.

Changes in one's life may be expected—such as having one's children grow up and leave home—or unexpected—such as losing a job one considered secure. Illness may strike someone in the family. A move to a different part of the country may become necessary. At this time, in most communities, anxiety about sufficient family income has grown to gigantic proportions. However, there are also positive changes, such as completing a course of training and making a new start. An illness may be cured or an uncertainty removed. Many people who dream of winning a lottery are unaware that even this exciting event has an unsettling quality about it that may change one's inner self as much as one's circumstances.

Changes to the Earth's environment are very disturbing. It is not just a matter of the supply of fish, or the demand for wheat, ore, fur, or lumber. We are threatened by changes in the quality of basic aspects of nature: the depletion of the ozone layer makes the sun a dangerous necessity of life; pollution of the air will make it increasingly difficult for all of us to breathe. Many communities are faced with a choice between challenging un-scrupulous businesses that pollute or deplete their environment, or keeping the jobs these businesses provide. This is hard. But the changes in people may be difficult, too. Many of the old familiar people feel "lost" amid the influx of a new style of person or family. Communities that formerly felt so comfortable and safe can begin to feel like foreign countries in which we, and our accustomed ways, seem to be under attack—or at least questioned. This is extremely unsettling.

What starts a process of growth in faith, particularly when there is no evidence of an external "cause," is the subject of much debate. Many who have completed extensive research on this matter, such as James W. Fowler, believe that growth in faith is a natural part of human development—like having permanent teeth replace baby ones.[1] Others vigorously deny this possibility. I believe that the normal process of maturing offers possibilities for many kinds of change, both good and bad. I believe that God is involved with the whole of life and is therefore able to enter our lives at any time and place, in any way in which we allow God to do so. We are simply sometimes more open to matters of the spirit.

If there are no dramatic events such as a death or an economic recession to deal with, a searcher begins by asking questions. According to Westerhoff and Willimon, the questions have a predictable pattern.[2] One questions others first, then one's own self, and finally the tradition that has shaped the faith and practice of one's faith community. Doubts may arise and be very painful. Others may not appreciate having questions raised and will try to give quick and easy answers or otherwise silence the questioner. One of the characteristics of the community faithstyle is that it is often unwilling to allow questions or investigations or experiments with alternatives, the very things that searchers need.

Searchers give recognizable clues as to what is happening to them. These clues are given in tentative statements in the beginning stages: "Have you ever wondered...?"; "Sometimes I think that..."; "It hardly seems possible that..."; "Wouldn't it be great if...?" are favourite expressions. Later on, the tone may change: "I simply don't believe that Jonah was swallowed by a whale!"; "Welcoming only people like ourselves to church is evil!"; "We need to study that before shooting our mouths off!" Other church members may be put off by such statements, and either fight or isolate the searcher. A great number of searchers may subsequently either leave that church or just keep quiet. This is tragic, not only for them, but for the whole congregation. The searchers' gifts go unacknowledged, and their personal growth in relationship with God may be hampered. Given free rein, the choice of a searcher is to search—to find his or her own answers, to understand, to really grasp what their faith is all about and how it may be lived in a way that is satisfactory for them.

A diagram of a searcher's explorations might look something like this:

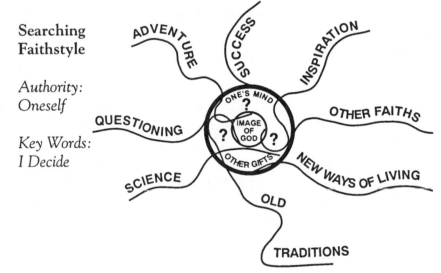

Searching Faithstyle

Authority: Oneself

Key Words: I Decide

I realize fully that community faithstyle persons, and others who read this, may think, "The poor things—looking in all the wrong places." Whereas the image of God at the centre is always in interaction with the person in the community faithstyle, the searcher is isolated from that centre. One's mind and other gifts may be operating, but the "God-connection" is what the search is all about. Those who get stuck in the searcher style may become agnostics (who don't believe that we can really know God) or rationalists (thinking that one's mind, including science and technology, is what really matters). Needless to say, searchers can be opposed to some institutions of religion and may even become active in anti-institutional activities.[3]

M. Scott Peck makes an interesting observation about searchers: "One of the greatest challenges, in fact, facing the church is how to facilitate the conversion from Stage II to Stage IV without them having to spend a whole adult lifetime in Stage III." In my terms, this means that community faithstyle persons may move into searching and become permanently stuck. Peck goes on to say: "As far as I am concerned, one of the two greatest sins of our sinful Christian Church has been its discouragement, through the ages, of doubt."[4] He points out that this discouragement has both driven people away from the church and made them resistant to spiritual insights.

Within the small community faithstyle church, however, it may not be easy to accept doubters and critics. One person's doubt may set off a whole chain reaction of doubt and fear among persons already over-stressed. It is not surprising that an effort may be made to silence the doubter. Faith is seen by many to be an acceptance of an established system of beliefs, not an ongoing process. It is hard to be sensitive to the needs of one who is disturbing all the others. Yet searchers need encouragement rather than condemnation. As the search goes on, there may be growing recognition that God works in doubt as well as in certainty. If others in the community could affirm that truth, it would help everyone to be more free and confident in their faith. It would help everyone to feel that they are valued as whole persons and not just as workers in the community.

Many community faithstyle persons staunchly believe that our national churches and councils of churches are "off the mark" altogether in their involvement with social justice issues.

They argue that the church's job is personal conversion. The converted person will then work through other agencies to effect necessary social adjustments. There is some validity to the argument that we in the churches have not worked sufficiently on spiritual development. To a frightening extent, we have been more concerned about the church's survival. We have even used social justice issues—reaching out to the poor or the starving, for example—as tools to increase church interest and attendance. Some of us are drawn to such activities for humanitarian rather than spiritual reasons. Many searchers are most comfortable when their faith is not questioned or required in order for them to be part of a caring community. Congregations really need to understand what their goals are in order to handle the variety of faith needs in their members and adherents.

One searcher described her church's worship services to me: "They sing the same songs, at the same pace, as they did when I was a child. The minister drones on without any chance for anyone to comment or question. They insist that we take cookies to things and work like mad for 'The Supper.' They give to missions to convert 'the heathen' and never *think* about their own faith and whether their lives reflect what they claim to believe when they are in church." This searcher made two other interesting comments: "Our church has been really good for this community," and "I'm going, when I can, to a place where it is not assumed that I believe everything the leaders believe, where I get to express my own opinions."

Searchers *analyze* the difference between the sociological sense of community and the church sense of community at an early stage of their questioning. They ask, What is different about the church? Is it simply a cog in the machine that includes the school and sports and social events, the council and other governments? In *Land and Community*, Alex Sim gives a socio-logical analysis of vertical and horizontal organizations. The church is both a vertical (local) and horizontal (widespread) organization. Sim speaks of the "branch plant mentality" of horizontal organizations. He states that the church is "the hardiest of all institutional perennials," partly because of its local tradition and powers. Yet policies set by the central office often ignore important facts about local realities.[5]

Sim has a profound sense of the loss of power in rural communities now—and not only rural ones. When I read the following paragraph, I realized how widely the words apply:

Clearly, decentralization should be the order of the day as far as rural communities are concerned, yet the urge to decentralize is ... blunted by the people themselves. Many of them no longer believe their opinions or efforts can make the slightest difference in the affairs of state or even in their own community. This is a tragic condition—to feel alienated in one's own country, or worse, in one's own community. There is a tendency to blame individuals for inertia and refusal to accept social responsibility, but surely the trend toward more and more centralization in the control of social and political affairs contributes largely, though of course not exclusively, to increasing alienation. Passivity is encouraged by families where decisions are "handed down" and by schools with rigid curricula and supervisory techniques. Then there is television, where canned hilarity tells us when to laugh and the commercial tells us what to wear, what to eat and what to drink.[6]

In my mind's eye, I see another searcher, an older person, sitting in her kitchen on a sunny day. She talks about the God-given order and beauty she sees in creation around her and of her community's confusion and pain. "We really fought the closing of our local school. We did everything we could. But it was closed. And now—now we wonder why we fought it. It seems to work all right as it is. Probably the change we are fighting now will go through, no matter what we do, and we'll accept it like we did the consolidation of schools. It hardly seems worthwhile to try to do anything. It will probably be a wasted effort." This searcher deeply appreciated the power of God in nature. She experienced the powers of government as alien and, in many cases, not related to community needs. The lack of harmony hurt her because she felt that communities of the past were really more of a natural expression of the life and values of the community members.

Because searchers are willing to study, experiment, and work towards broad goals, they perform a very significant role in both their local community and church. I have attended church meetings, however, where a searcher has made a simple proposal that began with, "Why do we always...?" The others in the group wrote him off, as if he were a child continually asking, "Why?" Power structures and brokers are often revealed on such occasions. Searchers soon learn that some church persons have invested a great deal of themselves and their family pride in "keeping up the tradition."

Sim states that the church has endured partly because of

> its combined and contradictory functions of conservation and tradition, as well as by personal and social renewal.... People return to it for the reassurance of familiar symbols, sounds, and sacraments. The church survives change and revolution by stubborn resistance and subtle compromise; at the same time its doctrines contain seeds of social and political criticism that often run counter to prevailing policies and practices.[7]

Searchers are likely to spot the contrasts and often stay in a church where they see some hope of change actually occurring.

Today, the church is trying to sort out what is essentially Christian and what people really believe to be contained in their "faith." I am concerned that we not try to push everyone into one straitjacket of doctrine. My research has made it abundantly clear that no one fits into a rigid category for a whole lifetime—no matter how much someone may pretend to do so. For example, I remember a strong community faithstyle parishioner who held a powerful position in a local church. She was never questioned except, perhaps, for advice on how to live as a Christian. One day, however, she spoke of a period in her life when she "just had to keep studying ... had to know everything." She "couldn't get satisfied." I inquired into what had happened at the end of this period. In terms of my three styles of faith, she had made the transition to "partner." But she habitually presented the community faithstyle front, because it was acceptable to her family and her friends in the community. Sadly enough, her community never profited as much as it could have from her searching and the deeply satisfying companionship with God that enriched her life.

As families have varieties of experiences with growth and change, so the faith community should expect to have unpredictable growth and change over the years. No one would argue that such transitions can be difficult, whenever they occur. However, we have the assurance that God is with us, even though we may not be aware of God at all in the middle of a search.

Questions to Consider

1. Do you believe that searching would be (or is) satisfying or scary?
2. What would it be like to make other people uncomfortable because you saw things in a different light?
3. Do you feel sorry for those persons who stop living in the "old ways"? If not, what do you feel?
4. Is there any way we can help the searchers in our midst?

Chapter Three

The Partnership Faithstyle

> *One in whom persuasion and belief*
> *Had ripened into faith, and faith become*
> *A passionate intuition.*
>
> William Wordsworth,
> "The Excursion," bk. vi

The partnership faithstyle is the most difficult to identify among the three styles. Many of the words and ideas are often similar to the other styles. This is not surprising, because the partnership style is, in essence, an integration of the two. A diagram of the style looks like this:

Partnership Faithstyle

Authority:
God and Self

Key Words:
Open to
the Spirit

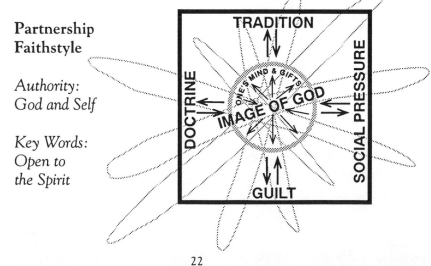

Partners have frequently outgrown rebellious feelings towards, or questioning of, the community faithstyle. They have
become able to appreciate its values and do not feel it necessary
to destroy traditional institutions. They have, instead, some
understanding of the importance of keeping the good qualities
while working to change the things that hindered them in
finding God's will. Like Nana in the introduction, they are able
to understand all points of view. Frequently, they take on the role
of peacemakers and peacekeepers of congregations.

Partners have found God, or been found by God. As Peck
reminds us, a change from one style to another is accompanied
by "a sense on the part of the persons converted that their own
conversions were not something they themselves achieved, but
rather gifts from God."[1] The change may happen very gradually
or extremely quickly. One of the ways in which we describe
becoming a "partner" is to say that we have become "whole."
Think about that. The two parts of our background—the "just
accept" of the received tradition *and* the "show me it makes
sense" of caution—are reconciled. Parts of each that are no
longer of use to us are put aside in order to let a new life of faith
grow within us. Large numbers of people have had this experience. It is not an experience that one can maintain at the same
high level of conviction or feeling all of the time, but the
strength of it often becomes a reassuring underlying base for life.
Blaise Pascal wrote of such an experience:

> The year of our Lord 1654.
> Monday, 23 November,
> from about half past ten
> in the evening until about
> half past twelve at night: fire.
> God of Abraham,
> God of Isaac,

God of Jacob,
not the God
of philosophers and scholars.

Certainty, joy, peace.
God of Jesus Christ.
He is only found along the ways
that are taught in the gospel.

Tears of joy.
I had parted from him.
Let me never be separated
from him.
Surrender to Jesus Christ.[2]

Not everyone has such a dramatic encounter with God. For some there are experiences of a slowly developing peace and security about God and a knowledge of who Jesus Christ really is. Many speak of reading the Bible and beginning to feel that "that's really true for me." Some have experiences in groups or with another person that help move them to greater depths of feeling and understanding. Some come to faith through battle— with alcohol or drugs, with depression, with a co-worker one can't stand, a loss that seems too great to be borne.

When writing a thesis on women's roles in abortion decisions, I read widely of literature from around the world. I was struck by how many persons found that making an unavoidable decision, one that affected their deepest reality, could simultaneously be an occasion for meeting God. In the most extreme conditions, many people felt met by a love that affirmed their own being and connected them to the deepest truth. This usually happens only when a person is allowed to make her or his own decision and take responsibility for it. This is significant in terms of "community faithstyle decisions," which tend to be made by applying a blanket rule regardless of the unique inner reality of the person most directly involved.

In a community faithstyle group, or even a searcher group, it may be very easy to simply do what one is advised to do instead of what one believes is right for one's own self. There is a special quality to decision making in the partnership faithstyle. The base is an earnest and deep seeking to know God's will. It is not just a matter of "feeling good about it"; it is a matter of feeling that "it is right" for oneself at this time. When that conclusion is reached, action can be taken with peace. Persons in the other styles may also do this, of course, especially if they have a practice of regular prayer and meditation.

A pastor recently reported an experience shared by a married woman in her congregation. She and her family had decided that having another baby did not make sense for them in view of their job losses and money problems. So she made an appointment to have an abortion. As she sat in the waiting room, she became aware that her understanding of the situation was changing. She felt "sure that it was right" for her to carry the baby after all, and she was confident that things would work out for her family. She was now at peace, and her husband accepted her decision. All went well and everyone was delighted with the outcome.

There are now more and more people facing important decisions in which "voices" conflict. In *Sowing Circles of Hope*, a booklet of stories collected by Ollie Miller from support groups for older farm women in Saskatchewan, people struggle with family and community needs as well as their own. If older persons wish to leave their farm and move into a nearby town, the incomes and lifestyles of all family members must be considered. Health needs may dictate a move to a place that has good facilities and services available. However, when it comes right down to it, how one values one's own self is an extremely crucial question. A sign of this may be whether or not a widow co-signs a farm loan with her son. The community faithstyle training tends to assume that "of course one would. Carrying on the farm tradition is a central value in this family's life. And we have to keep our community going if we can." The unwritten and unspoken part of that is, "Don't be selfish."[3]

The searcher faithstyle person might make lists of arguments both for and against and solicit advice from "experts." That may be wise in any case, but the important question here is: "Have I the right to make up my own mind?", immediately followed by: "Have I the courage to carry out what I decide to do if someone disagrees or is hurt or punishes me for it?" To think independently may be a hard thing to do in these circumstances. A person might know very well what is best in a practical sense, but be overwhelmed by other considerations.

The partnership style person comes at the question in another way. God's partner asks: "What is the best course for us in this situation?" *All* the people involved have value, the traditions have value, the facts have value. However, when it comes right down to it, the decision may be made after much prayer and meditation, as well as discussion and fact finding. I have found that when decisions have to be made, there is a time when a course becomes clear, when I no longer feel tension in my stomach as I think about it, and when it feels *possible* to do it— even if it will be hard. It is important to note that deep feelings need to be recognized and worked through before this can occur.

Partners make time to be with God. So do community faithstyle persons, of course. What distinguishes the two is often a difference in attitude. Community faithstyle persons often relate to God as to a highly honoured boss. Partners relate to God as co-workers in life. They talk things over. They wait for answers. They both love God and receive God's love in a way that gives purpose and direction to their lives. Community faithstyle persons are more likely to have that sort of feeling about Jesus, and that can be very helpful. When a decision is made, however, it is important who takes the responsibility.

Some people say, "God, or Jesus, told me to do it." Partners are more likely to report: "I spent a lot of time with God and have decided that it is best to...." The reality is that God does communicate with us in significant ways, if we allow it. It takes some practice and some courage, but it is a big help in times of trouble and uncertainty.

We also need to talk with others. As Ollie Miller found, this is not always easy. Some persons believe that they should keep their troubles to themselves and work them out alone. Certainly it is not wise to pour everything out to just anyone: we need to share with someone who cares for us and will treat our confidences with respect. We forget who we are, in a sense, if we do not have such communication. I do not mean just sharing "the news" with someone. I mean sharing something of who we really are. This, believe it or not, may also be an important way of being with God. Piri Thomas writes of his experience in a jail cell:

> I went back to my cell....
> The night before my hearing,
> I decided to make a prayer.
> It had to be on my knees....
> I couldn't play it cheap.
> So I waited until the thin kid was asleep,
> then I quietly climbed down from my top bunk
> and bent my knees....
>
> I knelt at the foot of the bed
> and told God what was in my heart.
> I made like He was there in the flesh with me.
> I talked to Him plain....
> No big words, no almighties....
> I talked to Him like I had wanted to talk
> to my old man so many years ago.
> I talked like a little kid and I told Him of

my wants and my lacks, of my hopes
    and disappointments.
I asked the Big Man … to make a cool way for me…
I felt like I was someone
who belonged to somebody who cared.
I felt like I could even cry if I wanted to,
something I hadn't been able to do for years.
"God," I concluded, "maybe I won't be an angel,
but I do know I'll try not to be a blank.
So in Your name, and in *Cisto's* [Christ's] name,
I ask this. Amen."

A small voice added another amen to mine.
I looked up and saw the thin kid, his elbows bent,
his head resting his hand.
I peered through the semidarkness to see his face,
wondering if he was sounding me.
But his face was like mine, looking for help from God.
There we were, he lying down,
head on bended elbows,
and I still on my knees.
No one spoke for a long while.
Then the kid whispered,
"I believe in *Dios* [God] also.
Maybe you don't believe it, but I used to go to church,
and I had the hand of God on me.
I felt always like you and I feel now,
warm, quiet, and peaceful,
like there's no suffering in our hearts."

"What's it called, Chico, this what we feel?"
I asked softly.

"It's Grace by the Power of the Holy Spirit,"
the kid said.

I didn't ask any more.
There, in the semidarkness,
I had found a new sense of awareness....[4]

We in the mainline churches sometimes have too much reserve for our own good. We need to share and pray together. We need to feel the effect of one of the most significant aspects of the partnership style—that sense of peaceful warmth that gives us meaning at the depth of our being. To the degree that we keep partnership faithstyle persons quiet in our congregations, we shut off these opportunities, God's gifts—freely offered to us all.

Partnership faithstyle persons who are welcoming and hospitable add another dimension to our lives. They are generally able to accept others—even those very different from themselves—as being God's people too. This means that the circle of those they care about is enlarged. Community faithstyle persons tend to maintain literal area and family boundaries. Searcher faithstyle persons tend to have educational and discussion boundaries. Partnership style persons, because they are connected with God at a deeper level, more readily connect with more of God's people and God's creation. They enlarge our vision and give us hope of more peace in our world.

Questions to Consider

1. Do you know any partnership faithstyle persons? If so, how do you feel about them? Are you such a person? If not, would you like to be?
2. Does it make a difference to your group and/or congregation if what God may want is considered rather than only what will please the group?
3. Does the idea of being so close to God feel good to you?
4. What differences would there be in your group and/or congregation if there were more active partnership persons in it?

II

EXPERIENCING THE FAITHSTYLES

Chapter Four

Ideas of God

God, The All Powerful

Our God's a fortress firm and sure,
a strong defence around us.
With him we know our cause secure,
though griefs and pains surround us.

Martin Luther,
The Hymn Book, #135

Imagine yourself as a child again. You are being told about God. What sort of image did you form from the information you received? The following are commonly reported:

- God was like a great big Daddy who sat on a throne in a celestial palace.
- God had lots of servants to do what he wanted.
- God could make things just by saying, "Let there be…"
- God sometimes became angry and did terrible things like killing people in plagues or floods or other disasters.
- God promised with a rainbow that floods, such as the one

Noah experienced, would never come again.
- God chose some people to have all the good land but didn't care about the people without land at all.
- Sometimes God chose a bad person to do what he wanted—like Jacob.
- Sometimes God let good people get killed—like Jesus.
- People tried to keep God happy and be friends with God, but God couldn't be trusted to do what you wanted or needed.
- People tried to understand God, but that was impossible.

If all this sounds confusing, contradictory, and only a little bit of the whole story of God, it is meant to. As children, we had some strange ideas about God. Many of us were taught the "Now I lay me down to sleep" prayer, with its infamous line, "If I should die before I wake, I pray the Lord my soul to take." A fear of God, and sometimes confusion about what a soul is, were often caused by these words—although some adults still find the prayer comforting. When a person died, even a parent, children were often told that God wanted them to be with him. God frequently was seen by children as unfair, a bully, and sometimes a murderer.

As such thoughts were not allowed, children had to praise God, give God glory, love and serve God, no matter what they thought. Think about that. Were you happy as a child with what you learned about God? If you raised questions, how were they treated? A common way in which questioning was handled in a community faithstyle group was telling a child that to question was a sin and could therefore bring punishment. Thus, children were expected to accept what they were told about religion as if it were a special kind of knowledge or experience. God became the Great Magician who rewarded good children and adults. If bad things happened to you, you must be bad. Is this what you were taught, the conclusion you reached?

The developmental damage caused by this repressive demand

is more apparent with today's knowledge of how a child's mind works. For example, if a child's parents separate, the child will often think that he or she has caused it by being bad. Children become angry with their parents for one reason or another and often misbehave, but they can easily imagine there is evil in these normal feelings and behaviours that could potentially harm or destroy good people. The ban on questioning and the stress on "being good" may have conspired to limit a child's ability to learn how to deal reasonably with life's events. The lesson commonly learned was that you must control yourself at all costs.

The following beliefs are the bedrock of faith for many community faithstyle persons: Human beings are basically evil; it takes a lot of hard training and discipline to become "good"; even if you are good, bad things can happen; God is "a jealous God visiting the iniquity of the fathers upon the children unto the third and fourth generation" (Ex. 20:5, KJV); thus, the eternal future of not only your own soul, but that of your descendants, is determined by your behaviour.

That God can do anything God pleases was rarely questioned. If you did not receive the recovery, the crop, or the peace you asked for, God was apparently teaching you a lesson. Given human nature, it was not hard to remember times when tempers were lost, greed experienced, or bad words said. God never missed anything. Some people even saw God as a dark shape waiting to pounce whenever a person sinned.

So where does this leave community faithstyle persons? One way that some deal with such teachings is to put God in a cage. Its walls are Sunday, Church, Bible, Prayer. They refuse to let God become a part of life in general. Like putting on your best clothes for church, these persons sometimes put on their religious faces and manners and go forth to "give unto the Lord the glory due unto his name" (Ps. 29:2, KJV). They hope that it will be enough to satisfy God and prevent interference in their lives.

Of course, there are others who live daily with God and rejoice in a relationship based on trust. "Though He slay me yet will I trust in Him," they say with Job (Job 13:15, *KJV*). We don't always realize that these people add something important to the belief that human beings are basically evil: they know that they can be forgiven. Such persons range from the charismatics who enthusiastically celebrate the work of the Holy Spirit to people who quietly, deep within themselves, know that Jesus Christ has set them free. Paul would say they have become friends with God (II Cor. 5:18, *TEV*).

Within the community faithstyle, however, as compared with the searching and the partnership faithstyles, God's action is stressed rather than seeking and/or finding through study and/or meditation. The all-powerful God is seen to be the giver of the good feelings and good things they enjoy. Questioning is done within carefully set limits, the answers accepted from a source declared trustworthy within the system. Personal analysis of the issue at stake is limited. "So far and no farther" is often a braking thought.

Within a community faithstyle group it is quite all right to have a Bible Study discussion about how God deals with us. However, it is not all right to ask, "Is there a God?" One searching person commented to a relative, "I wonder sometimes if there is a God." The immediate retort was, "What a ridiculous thing to say!" Any question about the nature of God thus questions the basis of the whole community faithstyle.

Because this basic assumption is not open to investigation, some persons are truly frightened by any deep questions or new experiences. Those who undergo a great tragedy, such as the lingering death of a child, for example, frequently report that they move out of step with others. Their feelings and thoughts are often seen by others within the community as needing "correction." They may drop out of their congregation and change friends. People of the community faithstyle generally

36

want re-affirmation of their basic belief system, not the risk of looking for a deeper understanding or experience of it. Those who have struggled deeply through force of circumstance often form a kind of underground network among community faithstyle groups. Sometimes they find help in groups for the bereaved or for separated spouses or for those whose lives have been affected by alcohol or drugs. The reassurance that such groups offer is that their feelings are okay and are not signs of impending eternal damnation.

We all know others who sail on smooth seas of contentment through a lifetime of community faithstyle religion. They have always known God as a loving Father. They have never experienced either shattering pain or exciting re-birth. They trust God and live with God in an uncomplicated way. God is as real to them as their own body and mind. They are often persons who, as children, were deeply loved at home and warmly welcomed in church and Sunday school. Their basic relationship to God was formed within a profound acceptance of their personhood as good and worthwhile. Among such persons, the dark side of the community faithstyle may never be experienced. They receive great comfort and meaning in this life and the assurance of eternal bliss to come.

Questions to Consider

1. Are any of your childhood ways of imagining God a part of how you think about God now?
2. What do you feel when you hear the phrase, "The fear of the Lord is the beginning of wisdom"? (Ps. 111:10, KJV)
3. How do you feel when or if someone seems to turn from God when he or she is in trouble?
4. Do you ever feel pressured to obey or believe something that your mind tells you is really questionable?

God, Who Wants to be Found

Nothing's so hard but search will find it out.

Robert Herrick,
Seek and Find

Searching for God can be either enjoyable or agonizing. If a person is prompted by a sense of curiosity and adventure, it is fascinating to discover the variety of ways in which people experience and describe God. For those who have lost someone or something dear to them, and who are frantically trying to get a handle on some reason to live, it may be frustrating to know that they are not the first ones to have sought explanations for the many mysteries of our universe and human life, which include God.

Christians belong to the Judeo-Christian tradition, which accepts the idea of God found in the Old and New Testaments of our Bible. This tradition teaches, among other things, that

- God is One and the Creator of the whole universe as well as of human beings;
- God created things and persons in a complex working system *that has meaning and purpose*;
- God did not set up the system and then sit back to watch it work—God is *involved*. The principles God intended for us to learn and live by can be discovered, and we can co-operate with them or not, as we choose;
- God is in favour of moral behaviour. People are held accountable for their actions;
- God *seeks a relationship with us*. This means that searchers are likely to *find* God if they search diligently.

Nevertheless, searchers frequently make the mistake of throwing the baby out with the bath water. They wipe out everything they have been taught or read or heard. They may find other faith traditions intriguing, or they may be drawn into New Age thinking. One of the shared characteristics of both Eastern religions and New Age practice is meditation. This is a link with spirituality that they may have missed in Christianity. If they follow any other faith tradition carefully, including New Age practices, they may come to a new understanding of some basic beliefs of Christianity and see its possibilities in a different light—or they may not!

A genuine searcher cannot escape a consideration of the basic question of whether there is a God and, if so, what relation God has, or desires to have, with human beings. Some New Age religious groups may tell the searcher, "You've got this search all wrong—you are already God in yourself. Why are you looking out there when you only need to look within?" This belief may be very appealing, as may its opposite extreme—accepting the ways of a cult and its leader as God. Searchers may also need to try on the idea that there is no God and no meaning anywhere for anybody—that life is just accidental.

In the past, many persons began their search when they first became involved with science. Evidence of the age of the universe can upset a childhood faith. However, confidence in the ability of the human brain to accomplish anything and everything needed, to explain all human behaviour and to be able to control it, has fortified the claims of science. It is only recently that scientists, reaching the limits of their knowledge, have admitted, "We know a lot about what happened, but we do not know the why of some of the fundamental things in the universe." James Fowler comments: "When the theoretical physicists begin to speak of a superforce—the combined and integrated effects of the four basic forces that maintain pattern and symmetry in the universe—it should not be surprising that a theologian thinks of the loving energy and unifying spirit of a creative God."[1]

Searchers frequently reject the image of the "All-Powerful God," who is seen as spying, condemning, ordering, and never to be questioned. If they analyze the matter, they may realize that this image of God makes them feel "put down" as persons. If their idea of God begins to accommodate Fowler's "loving energy," they will find evidence that there is obviously a much bigger, stronger, wiser, more tolerant, and more loving God involved in the universe. This is a God who functions, not out of human-style anger or need for control, but out of a meaningful, consistent centre of love and purpose. Fowler states that God invites human beings to share in the ultimate purposes of, not only human life, but that of the universe. This God does not give approval to all and "good luck," but works with us towards what is best for everyone. If searchers are looking for a magic wand to make all their dreams come true, they may be rudely disappointed.

The matter of self-worth is important. New Agers delight in the idea that God is within themselves, but they may not recognize that this can only be a tiny part of an infinitely greater God who created the whole universe and made us able to communicate with Godself. Christians believe that this God sent Jesus to be one of us, to both help us to understand and to empower us to have a different relationship with God. The prophets had spoken of a time when God's Spirit would be in people's hearts. Joel makes an important point for women who are conscious of the major role the Bible gives to men: "I will pour out my spirit on all flesh; your sons and your daughters shall prophesy…. Even on the male and female slaves, in those days, I will pour out my spirit" (Joel 2:28, NRSV). Everyone, no matter their natural gifts or worldly positions, may become aware of this Spirit and the possibility of speaking and acting for and with God. It's a whole new way of being in the universe.

Searchers seek to understand how injustices and wars can go on if God is a God who cares for human life and wants peace among us. It seems impossible that such a God, if this God really has any power, could allow the atrocities that we view on our television screens day after day. The image of the "All-Powerful God" seems to fail here, yet the possibility of good coming out of suffering needs to be remembered. Easter does follow Good Friday.

If a person is searching because he or she has lost a loved one, none of this may matter at all. The experience may consist of an intense need to make sense of what feels like total desolation. God may seem to be missing and be presumed dead. Other searchers, for other reasons, may have an equally tortured feeling. Mystics call this "the dark night of the soul." To some degree, and at some point in our lives, it happens to all of us. Many psalms deal with it, as in Psalm 102, paraphrased by Leslie Brandt:

> Good Lord, where are you?
> If you really do exist,
>   why don't you come out of hiding and do something
>   about this creature in distress?
> I am physically weary, I am mentally depressed,
> I am spiritually defeated.
> I can't eat, can't sleep.
> I am like garbage,
>   discarded refuse in the back alley;
>   like yesterday's newspaper
>   shuffled around by the wind.
> I feel like some sort of zombi,
>   some nonentity,
>   some nothing that people,
>   if they acknowledge,
>   would only curse.
> I eat crow and drink gall.
> Now even You have tossed me aside

like some moth-eaten garment
that no one could possibly want.

When someone is in the midst of such a "dark night," there are no easy answers, no quick solutions. If we have lost our love or our livelihood or our health, we have to reconstruct our lives. It helps if we have understanding persons to give us support. It helps, too, if we remember that God has not deserted us even if the shades are down. Psalm 102 reminds people of that. Brandt continues:

But the prophets have proclaimed Your name,
    and the Scriptures declare Your mercy,
    and the old saints pass on Your promises.
You do reign over our world, they say,
    You do show concern
    for the poor clods of this earth.
Good Lord, prove it!
Look down from wherever You are
    on Your creatures wallowing in wretchedness.
Deliver us, O God, set us free!

I must take comfort in Your everlastingness
    that You who outlive seasons and centuries,
        who have blessed the saints of the past,
    can also care for Your servants
in this fearful hour.
For Your years have no end,
    nor do the destinies of those who trust in You.[2]

One of the most helpful things about the Bible is its refreshing honesty about human feelings and actions. We catch glimpses of predicaments that recur in every generation. As we read Brandt's paraphrase of Psalm 102, we learn that it is perfectly all right to charge God with neglect and to have confused feelings about our situation. Searchers need to understand that this is a part of the work of searching—to battle through the doubts and fears, the feelings of rejection and loneliness when old, accepted truths are put aside. New insights come in their own time. They do not arrive fully developed and ready to be put into practice. We need to talk honestly with God even when we question whether or not God actually exists. Furthermore, we must remember that others have walked the same road, fought the same battles, and have come through to light and peace.

One of the most touching stories of searching is found in a poem by Francis Thompson, entitled "The Hound of Heaven." The story begins with:

> I fled Him, down the nights and down the days;
>   I fled Him, down the arches of the years;
> I fled Him, down the labyrinthine ways
>   Of my own mind; and in the midst of tears
> I hid from Him, and under running laughter.
>   Up vistaed hope I sped;
>   And shot, precipitated,
> Adown Titanic glooms of chasmed fears,
> From those strong Feet that followed, followed after.
>
>   But with unhurrying chase,
>   And unperturbéd pace,
> Deliberate speed, majestic instancy
>   They beat—and a Voice beat
>   More instant than the Feet—
> "All things betray thee, who betrayed Me."

The author pleads with God, looks to persons, especially children, for help, then looks to nature. At the end, God confronts him with information about his life and what has happened.

"All which I took from thee I did but take,
   not for thy harms,
But just that thou might'st seek it in My arms.
   All which thy child's mistake
Fancies as lost, I have stored for thee at home:
   Rise, clasp My hand, and come!"

"Halts by me that footfall:
   Is my gloom, after all,
Shade of His hand, outstretched caressingly?"[3]

Thompson is sharply aware of the searcher's fear that he or she will have to give up something treasured if they "surrender" to God. Old images may make the prospect uninviting. In the next section we look at what in fact happens if we take that inviting hand and allow God's love to bring us new insight, meaning, and joy. It is a whole different style of faith, which I call partnership.

Questions to Consider

1. Have you ever wondered if God *does* exist? If you have, what were the consequences? If not, have you ever had to stop yourself from wondering about it? Or has it simply never occurred to you to ask?
2. When you are really hurting, do you wonder if God is punishing you or if God just doesn't care?
3. When you think about the whole universe, do you ever wonder about your place in it? Does it matter to you?

God, The Partner in Life

*Thou hast made us for thyself, O Lord, and our heart
is restless until it rests in Thee.*

Without God, we cannot. Without us, God will not.

St. Augustine

The idea of being a partner with God may seem odd to some
persons, especially community faithstyle persons, who see God
as "wholly other" than themselves. In everyday life, partners
have some degree of equality. They have a different relationship
from, for example, an employer and an employee. Partners focus
on co-operation rather than obedience. They work towards the
same goal, using all available abilities.

James Fowler developed a theology of partnership based on
the idea that God created human beings to be the reflective part
of creation. It is possible for humans to grasp what life is about
and what needs to be done to fulfil God's purposes. Humans are
free to either work with God towards such purposes or not. God
offers a covenant relationship. This is neither an organic system,
such as a physical body, nor a contract, such as a state constitu-
tion. Rather, it is "a community called into being from beyond
itself."⁴ A real problem for many Christians today is the difficulty
in finding a community that believes it is "a community called
into being." Many churches function as institutions rather than
as places where people share and celebrate what God is doing
with them or calling them to do. This can be frustrating to those
who have connected with God at a deeper level.

Partners are those who have a deep and creative relationship
with God. This experience connects them to others in a new and
fresh way. They become brother and sister, equal recipients of
God's care. Therefore, they do not reach out to help others from
a sense of duty or limit themselves to giving only what is

required. To "brother" or "sister" your neighbour implies an openness to others, a sharing, as in a family where all are valued. It is this kind of relationship to which partners feel themselves called.

Partners discover that they need special nourishment to live according to this calling. A dedication made during a religious "high" can soon be lost if there is no one else to understand and affirm what has happened. Old habits can be strong and destructive. If someone shares their transformative experience and is told to forget it because the real world does not have room for that kind of thing, it can be devastating. Predominantly community faithstyle congregations are usually unable to accept and/or integrate such experiences because, for partners, authority has shifted from the community's traditions to a living, interactive God. Partners may need a lot of strength from elsewhere to survive in some churches.

Partners describe reading the Bible with "fresh eyes" as they move deeper into the style. They begin to identify with the purposes of God, to sense the frustration of wonderful possibilities when people go off on the wrong path, to share in the agony of God as people are tortured or denied justice. They begin to share the dream that peace may come as people gradually understand the possibility and change their ways. They begin to "brother" and "sister" instead of compete and betray. They seek to change society and their own lives to assist the movement towards life, justice, and peace for all.

The bedrock of a partner relationship with God is an openness to God in prayer and meditation. The channels that are a part of every human being gradually open wider, and the reality of God's loving purpose becomes clearer. Sometimes it is hard to believe that what is asked is possible. Partners are brought to an awareness of how much difference there is between God and human beings. As Isaiah puts it in 55:8: "... my thoughts are not your thoughts, nor are your ways my ways, says the Lord" (NRSV).

Jesus, as a human, knew that he had limits that God did not. He came to realize that he was going to be put to death and he struggled with that. Since the records were written so long after the actual events, we cannot know how much Jesus knew about what would happen to him. I believe that he came to a willingness to trust that God would use whatever happened for good, but that he was not certain of the details.

Partners understand that they share a calling—a vocation—to be part of God's unfolding plans for the world. There are certainly benefits for them, such as a life of deep meaning and joy, but they are not ends in themselves. Partners carry the vibrant energy of God into the world. It is not accidental that we sometimes speak of the results as "warmth" and "light." To bring "brother" and "sister" caring into a world obsessed with power and material objects is to bring a revolution. Partners delight in sharing the wonder of knowing God's love is for all—whoever and wherever they are.

Partners are not fixed in a particular way of thinking and doing. They may engage in searches of one kind or another as they encounter new challenges or new insights into God's work in the world. They often choose to enjoy the traditional faith practices, which may be a meaningful base for their spiritual life. Both community faithstyle persons and searchers have more limits. Daniel Day Williams, an early "process" theologian, comments:

> Among the many issues we follow one clue to the relation of the divine and the human loves. This is that all loves work within the history of the self's becoming. No love ... is a 'thing', a static pattern or form. It is a spirit at work in life and taking form in the process of becoming.[5]

A modern hymn by James K. Manley captures an aspect of the partner relationship with God as it relates to the world about us:

You call from tomorrow, you break ancient schemes,
from the bondage of sorrow the captives dream dreams;
our women see visions, our men clear their eyes,
with bold new decisions, your people arise.[6]

Questions to Consider

1. How do you feel about your relationship with God?
2. If God asked you to do something your fellow church members
   would disagree with, what would you do?
3. Do you really believe that God could consider you a partner?
4. Is the idea of a growing faith a pleasant one for you?

Chapter Five

Views of Creation

God's Work Begun

> *Thus says the Lord, your Redeemer,*
> *who formed you in the womb:*
> *I am the Lord, who made all things,*
> *who alone stretched out the heavens,*
> *who by myself spread out the earth....*
>
> Isaiah 44:24, NRSV

> *My purpose shall last; I shall do whatever I choose.*
>
> Isaiah 46:10, JB

In the beginning ... God created ... and God saw all that was done and declared it good. This is a basic belief of Christianity: the entire universe is God's design and handiwork and all that is in it is essentially good.

When we see beauty and experience growth and health in our world, we too say it is good. It lifts our hearts in wonder and appreciation. It re-affirms God's love for us as seasons come and go, our food is sown and harvested, our senses bring us pleasure.

It is hard when trouble comes to comprehend what could have possibly gone wrong and what our responsibility is for the new situation. If everything is "sent by God," should we not simply submit? If we have reached for too much, as it is said of Adam and Eve, should we be punished? How can a loving God allow terrible things to happen? Is it possible that God really does not care? Or is God unable to prevent troubles on earth?

Community faithstyle persons may wonder about such things, but they usually stop short of blaming God directly. Many have been trained in catechisms, such as The United Church of Canada's published version of 1944. The question is: "What is the work of providence?" The answer is: "The work of providence is God's upholding and governing all things so that they work together for His good purpose, and His caring for His people with such constancy that nothing, except sin alone, can separate them from His love."

Countless writers and thinkers have dealt with questions concerning God's care over the centuries. What follows is intended to promote thought, not to suggest answers that *should* be accepted. It is extremely important, especially during difficult times, for us to know what we believe about God's care and whether God has the power to help. It helps to talk about these things with others to clarify our own beliefs and share our insights with others who may also be wondering about what we can trust.

Our Judeo-Christian tradition teaches us that God made the universe with a wisdom far beyond ours. Medical science is still trying to unravel the mystery of how we are put together—and we are only one small part of creation. We keep on learning and improving our abilities to help, but we also make mistakes—as with thalidomide and nuclear waste. As twentieth-century Christians, we believe that God wants us to explore our world and ourselves, but we do not often receive simple, clear, helpful answers. We have to judge for ourselves. When even experts disagree, how can anyone know who or what to trust?

There are times when we know what we should do, but we do not want to do it or feel that we cannot. A good example is protecting our land and water from chemicals. Clearly the overall increase in population has put stress on our environment. Food is essential. So is money and a good distribution system. It is hard to see how something good for so many generations—like producing all the food we can—can have destructive side effects. If God has given us knowledge, should we not use it? What cost is reasonable for what we believe we need? Such questions are complicated and involve science, economics, and world conditions. People may feel betrayed when demands are made of them by others who may seem not to understand. No-till farming, for example, may be seen as a setback by farmers, rather than as progress, yet conservationists pressure them to adopt this technique. Some people believe that "if we only lived in the old ways, we would all be all right."

Community faithstyle persons may feel twinges of guilt about wanting too much or abusing resources, but their faith in God, the Creator who brings the seasons, assures them that this too will pass. Markets and growing conditions will be good again; life will go on as before; God is infinitely resourceful. For community faithstyle groups, the unchangeable God—the God who can do anything and is always present—is a required base for faith. Without this belief, they may see no hope. However, there is another side to consider. How could anyone imagine that God does not care about this complex, magnificent creation in which we find ourselves? How can we think that if we act outside of God's purpose for creation, there will not be a reckoning? Surely God is involved in new responses to the situations we create. God is also likely to have other plans we do not know of at the moment, which may make our lives very different.

During hard times, it may seem to community faithstyle people as if God has turned against them. Yet creation always follows its own principles. For example, over-fishing brings depletion of stock. This is a hard reality. Yet decisions made in government sessions or business boardrooms are equally able to create or destroy livelihoods, as quotas are matters of human negotiation. How we allow God's gifts to be used determines the life or death of our dreams and plans.

American poet Archibald MacLeish responded to pictures taken during space flights by writing: "To see the earth as it truly is, small and blue and beautiful in that eternal silence where it floats, is to see ourselves as riders on the earth together, brothers on that bright loveliness in the eternal cold—brothers who know now they are truly brothers."[1] If he were writing now he may have referred to "brothers and sisters." All of life is involved in sharing the space that exists on the skin of planet Earth.

This kind of thinking is a real challenge to some people. Canadians live in a vast, under-populated country, so that individualism was once a reasonable response—lots of land, lots of opportunity. However, the world has moved in on us—first with news reports on the radio, then pictures on television, and then real persons doing things that affect our lives. Competition in the markets where we sell our products has become a major issue and so has competition for our natural resources. All around the world, trade pacts are being negotiated as both the vision and the possibilities for production change. Multi-national companies plan globally, not locally. Their concern is with the "bottom line" of profit or loss, not with familiar neighbours or particular countries. The whole effect is both disorienting and frightening. People with "strange" ideas about the meaning of life and creation are making decisions with which we have to live!

Where is God in all this? For community faithstyle persons, God should make everything all right for those who trust and obey what their faith teachers taught them. More people are asking questions about the nature and intentions of God than they will admit. It is helpful for Christians to investigate the "bad times" in the Bible in order to see how they were handled by past believers.

Nehemiah 9:5-37 is a good example. When a bad time came, it was believed that people had not lived as they should. They needed to be punished by God and "brought into line." The Exile to Babylonia and the troubles that followed were therefore deserved. Yet this long historical psalm also celebrates God's loving care in the Exodus from Egypt and the settlement of the Promised Land. In verses 33, 36, and 37, we read:

> You [God] have been just in all that has happened to us, for you have shown your faithfulness, we our wickedness. Here we are now, enslaved; here in the land you gave our fathers to enjoy its fruits and its good things. We are slaves. Its rich fruits swell the profits of the kings whom for our sins you have set over us, who dispose as they please of our bodies and our cattle. Such the distress we endure! (JB)

No one trying to understand the attitudes of community faithstyle persons in difficulty can afford to overlook this view of the matter. It is part of our tradition.

Interestingly, Nehemiah 5:1-13 tells quite a different story. Those who loaned money to farmers for the purpose of re-establishing farming after the Exile forgave those debts, as the farmers were having to sell their sons and daughters into slavery. This is a plan of action many would like to put into practice today! Debts incurred in better times are major problems for more than farmers in our society. Even large property holders find themselves in trouble in times of economic recession or depression.

Nehemiah 9 describes a great ceremony where people acknowledged that they had sinned, where the re-discovered Book of the Law of God was read, and where a covenant was made to be faithful in the future by obeying the Word of the Law. This is an important ingredient in dealing with the grief of community faithstyle persons when they feel (whether or not anyone else considers it justified) guilty about something that has happened. This is sometimes referred to as "getting right with God." It involves a change in focus, if not of direction, that is centred on obedience to what is accepted as God's will. People often want to skip this step and turn immediately to applying practical solutions to the external problem, but for true community faithstyle persons, this is not satisfactory. The two aspects must be kept in balance.

Community faithstyle persons are most comfortable in an orderly, predictable society where everyone and everything has a clearly defined use, accepted by all generations. The turbulent nature of our times cannot be easy to accept. For example, the traditional role of men as the family breadwinners has made their usefulness clear to all for many generations. This image obscures the way in which rural women have traditionally gardened and produced much of the edible food for the family. Women have also worked in the fields, milked cows, prepared wool for clothing and bed-clothes. Both men and women worked directly with nature in past years to "get by" and maybe even "prosper." Now the situation is often that one or both works off the farm to earn enough income to merely survive. Men may find it extremely difficult to no longer be the traditional "breadwinners" in society's eyes. There may be some residual guilt associated with what they perceive as their failure to be men, which is reinforced by the traditional view of gender roles.

Urban families are also changing in what are sometimes dismaying ways. The high number of poor families headed by women means that many children are deprived of a father as well as the security of a comfortable home. This is a situation the Bible does not cover. Women were always attached to men—if not a husband, then a male relative.

Creation stories do not make "rules" regarding the traditional roles of men and women. Gifts are given to both sexes. Genesis 1:27 states clearly that male and female are both made in God's image. It is the older story of Adam and Eve that gives man first place. Even though Eve is brought into being as a "partner" for Adam (*NRSV*), the whole story of Adam being created first and Eve being formed, from his rib, to help him has given the impression of Eve as secondary.

Theologian Walter Brueggemann has written that men have often used both land and women to fulfil their economic and social dreams. This is contrary to the Bible's teaching that neither should be treated as a commodity, used and discarded or dominated to the extent that "life is squeezed out."[2] Both land and women have rights. This may sound strange to modern persons, but it points to a fundamental fact of creation—that life renews itself when proper care is taken of its source. These sources need to be respected for their intrinsic worth. This attitude may irritate women who know that they are much more than a source of life in our society, but it needs to be taken into account. The problem of infertility affects many couples, and dramatic technologies are being designed to make parenthood possible. Brueggemann suggests that such a situation results when women are misused. The creation God has given us is capable of better life possibilities.

Today's moral and ethical questions about the use of God's creation are different from what they used to be both for individuals and for society as a whole. We are at risk now of destroying nature as we know it as we continue to poison our land, water, and air. We have to begin a process of asking whether what is possible is also right or wise, and then find ways of curtailing damage so that life in all its forms is protected.

Farmers are changing their methods in light of environmental concerns. They use less commercial fertilizer, insecticides, fungicides; crop rotation is being used to control erosion; no-till practices are increasing. All of these are aimed at long-range conservation of the fertility of the land. Industrial practices are also changing. Pollution of air, land, and water is being vigorously attacked by many governments in order to prevent problems. We are gradually coming to understand how delicate some of the balances in creation are and how we may destroy ourselves if we destroy them.

Our planet has proven to be richly endowed with possibilities—including the possibility of its own destruction if some of its ingredients are put together in a certain way. The magnitude of human responsibility is gradually being seen in its true light. For community faithstyle persons, the effects may be too frightening to think about, let alone accept. Some pull back from it all and choose to live in the old ways, by the old beliefs. This is certainly understandable. But others begin to search and the next section will explore that faithstyle.

Questions to Consider

1. The world as you see it is: (a) beautiful; (b) productive; (c) threatened; (d) purposeful; or (e) other.
2. If we get into trouble, have we brought it on ourselves? Does it matter if we were aware that we were doing something risky?
3. What does God do when we do things that are against God's purposes?
4. Does MacLeish's idea of our planet Earth (see p. 52) make God seem closer or farther away? What about other people?

God, the World, and Us

God who spoke in the beginning,
forming rock and shaping spar,
set all life and growth in motion,
earthly world and distant star;
he who calls the earth to order
is the ground of what we are.

F. H. Kaan,
The Hymn Book, #95

Searchers are prompted by a need to reject ideas about life, meaning, and God that they have been taught or have experienced. They may begin searching because of their dissatisfaction with the quality of the church services available to them or because their world has disintegrated through personal tragedy. There are all kinds of roads to the deep questioning that invites searchers to look at everything through fresh eyes and new feelings.

Kaan's faith, as exemplified above, requires a trust that our universe was created intentionally by a Creator who relates directly to us humans. Science has taught the searcher about the Big Bang theory of creation and the eons of time that passed while the planet Earth developed. Genesis 1 and 2 may seem like nonsense to the searcher. Instead of rejecting only the "days," a searcher may reject the idea that there is a Creator God who makes God's nature known to us if we allow it. In addition, searchers are often influenced by the pervasive cynicism that refuses to accept that there is anything meaningful beyond the uncertainties of political, economic, and ecological problems.

Searchers look for evidence. They may do in-depth studies of the Bible and other scriptures. They may read related material by atheists or agnostics. They may get involved in discussions of various kinds, with a variety of people. At some points, they may feel a bit like a sponge, soaking up all the information they can find. They process everything through all their past beliefs and experiences. They may scoff at what they see as simple-minded thinking, as in Kaan above, or in the traditional spiritual, "He's got the whole world in his hands." If the very existence of God is in question, the idea of a personal God who cares for us individually is too much even to consider!

Many people are untrained in the Christian faith's traditions. They may not know the Bible. They may not realize that the idea of God grew slowly over centuries of experience with actual lives and events. There is a remarkable development in the Hebrew faith around the time of the Exile, for example. The popular song "By the Rivers of Babylon" reminds those familiar with Psalm 137 of the agony of loss when the exiles were taken to a strange land. They thought they had lost their God—that God resided only in their own territory. "By the rivers of Babylon—there we sat down and there we wept when we remembered Zion"; "How could we sing the Lord's song in a foreign land?" (vs. 1,4, NRSV). The Psalm ends with a note of vengeance: "Happy shall they be who pay you back what you have done to us! Happy shall they be who take your little ones and dash them against the rock!" (NRSV).

Then the prophets began to be heard. They were listening to God and receiving a very different message. Their God was with them. God was working out a purpose. God cared about all the world and all people. People sin and suffer, but that is not the whole story. Hosea 11:3,4 says: "... it was I [God] who taught Ephraim to walk, I took them up in my arms; but they did not know that I healed them. I led them with cords of human kindness, with bands of love. I was to them like those who lift infants to their cheeks. I bent down to them and fed them" (NRSV). Isaiah gives us the wonderful promise of "the suffering servant" who will bring forgiveness through his pain: "by his bruises we are healed" (Isa. 53:5, NRSV). To Christians, Jesus is the fulfilment of this vision. Isaiah 54:5 tells us "the Holy One of Israel is your Redeemer, the God of the whole earth he is called."

If we think about such developments in the biblical story, we realize that searchers—who look deep into the present for its meaning and think of its future possibilities—have an important role to play in connecting everyday life with the life that may be possible now and in the future. In other areas of life, it has been searchers who have made the scientific discoveries that underlie our modern lifestyle. They looked for answers to questions or problems and found that the universe has governing laws that may be used for all sorts of things. They also realized that these laws cannot be ignored. You cannot succeed in flying an aircraft if you do not understand the force of gravity, for example. In the same way, God has laws or principles that govern God's connection with human beings, which we ignore at our own peril. Searchers seek these out amid all the accumulations of religious institutions and practices. They seek the core of the matter and then work through to what is a reasonable response to the truth they have found.

I once worked in a Sunday school with a brilliant surgeon. He told me that medical doctors tend to either reject religion outright or take it seriously and want it to be all that it promises. Half-way measures or lukewarm conformity to the traditions do not invite their participation. Sunday after Sunday, over a hundred of our teenagers received a genuine personal witness from this man, as well as faith teachings. He had completed a vigorous search and found a deep meaning that affected all of his life. A nurse who worked with him told me of a night when he had operated on a boy with a ruptured appendix. When the surgery was over, she found the surgeon on a balcony looking at the stars and praying for the boy and his family. He once told me that a problem with patients was that they sometimes had too much trust in doctors and treatments. He used this appendectomy as an example of a time when parents were sure that their son would be fine and he felt that only the power of God, added to his skill, would bring recovery.

Too often we forget the immense power of God to influence our lives. Like the reality of gravity in the scientific world, the reality of God's purposes needs to be explored and accepted as a basis for further understanding. So long as a searcher clings to a primitive or superstitious idea of God, she or he will not be free to explore the ways in which God truly does interact with us. If something is not reasonable, a searcher will usually reject it. If we want to help with the search, we need to be willing to look beneath the surface for the working principles. God may seem to be unpredictable at times. Some people live and some die, some people are flooded out and some are left intact, some people have easy lives and others keep getting hurt. We do not often see justice as an ordinary part of human life.

Searchers may be helped by a study or discussion with a knowledgeable person about the ways in which such questions have been handled through the centuries. The classical name for the related Christian doctrine is "The Providence of God." This has been explained in many ways, the most familiar being the idea that God "provides" what we need, as expressed, for example, in the historic Heidelberg Catechism. The trouble with this idea is that it does not often ring true to a person experiencing crisis or difficult times.

In an article entitled "The Question of the Doctrine of Providence," theologian Charles M. Wood states that the Providence of God doctrine is questionable, despite the fact that so many Christians believe in it or feel that they ought to believe in it. Consequently, many non-Christians "simply take this to be the common teaching of Christian churches on this point." Wood provides a valuable insight for searchers: he indicates how, at the theological level, Christian teaching may be changed, beginning with the question of whether something is true based on the criterion of personal experience.[3]

Question 27 of the Heidelberg Catechism is: "What do you understand by the providence of God?" The answer: "The almighty and ever-present power of God whereby he still upholds, as it were by his own hand, heaven and earth together with all creatures, and rules in such a way that leaves and grass, rain and drought, fruitful and unfruitful years, food and drink, health and sickness, riches and poverty, and everything else, come to us not by chance but by his fatherly hand."

The answer to the next question, "What advantage comes from acknowledging God's creation and providence?", is: "We learn that we are to be patient in adversity, grateful in the midst of blessing, and to trust our faithful God and Father for the future, assured that no creature shall separate us from his love, since all creatures are so completely in his hand that without his will they cannot even move."[4]

This catechism was called "the most ecumenical of the confessions of the Protestant Churches" by its translators, Miller and Osterhaven. Yet Wood states that "there appears to be a profound dissonance between what the Heidelberg Catechism commends to us and what many of us find ourselves able to understand or willing to affirm." Such doctrines are not able "to function fittingly as instruments of Christian understanding." He concludes his article by stating that

> there is sufficient promise in the concepts underlying the traditional affirmations to make the task of critical reappropriation and renovation worthwhile. At the same time, I am convinced that the result of such work will be, and should be, a doctrine of providence different in some important respects from what we have inherited.[5]

Searchers are delighted to know that such work is going on. They need to be reminded that Christians are able to study the implications of past formulations of their faith and consider how circumstances and the meaning of language have changed since the time they were written. For example, the idea of everything "[coming] to us not by chance but by [God's] fatherly hand," may, in contemporary terms, make us seem like "innocent victims." The traditional teaching that "we are to be patient in adversity, grateful in the midst of blessing, and to trust our faithful God and Father for the future" may make us doubt that we are capable of using our own strength and wisdom to improve our lives. Yet the assurance of God's loving care, which underlies both these statements, is a valuable affirmation of God's relationship with us. It is the idea of our being no more than recipients that is unacceptable to many people today—and not only to searchers!

Searchers can upset others because they often deal with really basic questions. They force us to re-think our faith. As many of us simply do not like to think, searchers may often feel lonely or rejected in regular mainline churches. They seek others who are like-minded when they can.

A worthwhile exercise for everyone is to think about how you came to have the faith you do or why you have abandoned what you may have had or why you have never been involved with any religious faith at all. Something has "instructed" all of us about how we came to be and what meaning our lives have—or may have. We do not have to be imprisoned by past understandings. Searching can be enormously interesting and fruitful, and should be encouraged in us all.

Questions to Consider

1. Are you happy in your present beliefs?
2. Does the idea of searching for the meaning of basic things please you? Make you afraid? Challenge you?
3. Does it matter what we believe about how the universe came to be?
4. Does it matter whether you believe that your life has another dimension of meaning beyond your everyday concerns?

Being a Meaningful Part of Creation

*Our minds are stopped at the miracles around us—
of birth, of color and sound, of the human mind, of
the stars in the Universe. We can only stand in awe,
wonder and humility that we are charged with the
safekeeping of our earthly home and its creatures—
perhaps even with the evolution of the planet Earth.*

Verna Ross McGiffin,
In Search of Wisdom, 95

Verna Ross McGiffin, when she was over eighty years old, wrote a marvellous little book about her life journey called *In Search of Wisdom: The Joy of Seeing through Old Illusions.* It is about being a person in our world. I had the privilege of visiting her together with a friend of mine some years ago to learn how to work on personal development in small communities. From her I also learned about living with intense pleasure from and interest in the natural world around us.

Verna was caring for an injured bird, hundreds of miles from its homeland. It had collapsed on her lawn while barely alive. We speculated on why, in what may have been its dying moments, it kept on flying until it found the place where help was available. Neither Verna nor I had difficulty with the idea that there are possibilities of communication among different species like birds and animals and humans. We all belong to God's creation. We are all connected by levels of communication far beyond even our latest technological inventions.

Some urbanites may scoff at this idea; those who have lived and worked with nature probably have stories of their own to tell. Whether we are out on the ocean watching whales and dolphins, in the depths of a forest, aware of soft scurrying of small animals and the singing of birds, or ploughing good land, ready for seeding on a fine day, we may feel connected with life in all of creation. We may feel one with other creatures who are, like us, made by God's design and will. Aboriginal people have much to teach us about how to live with awe and wonder.

Partnership faithstyle persons are likely to be interested in and feel such connections. As Verna puts it: "All creatures are nourished by the soil and all return to it. Then we, and all creatures of earth, are the children of the mountain and siblings of each other."[6] This adds another dimension to the questions regarding the care of earth, air, and water. Partners ask, "What else is affected?" and "Who might be hurt?" as plans are considered. As part of the "family," they seek to protect life. This quality distinguishes partners from activists who operate from a different and sometimes non-religious perspective.

Nature helps us to understand ourselves. In many ways we find our limits when we confront its power. We cannot ignore how a tree falls when it is cut in a specific place, how refuge must be sought if a storm comes up at sea, how land has to "feel right" in one's hands in order to plough and seed successfully—even with computerized instruments. We find out how advantageous it is to co-operate with nature, and not only in practical terms. For William Wordsworth, nature is "the anchor of my purest thoughts.... and soul of all my moral being."[7] So can it be for us. Nature sets limits that cannot be broken: we may fly up into the sky, but we can never bring the beautiful clouds down to earth. We are, and they are, and the possibilities are limited by the nature of each.

The things we can do with nature through our technological and industrial advances are really quite remarkable, such as maximizing the number of calves from a prize cow by taking her eggs, fertilizing them in test tubes, and implanting them in a lesser grade of cow for gestation. We do miraculous things with computers in most businesses and keep on designing increasingly more "intelligent" ones. The computer on which I wrote this book is an IBM compatible. My nephew, an engineer, tells me that it is more logical than some. I believe it! I have to keep reminding myself that it always operates in a completely rational way—and that I do not. However, what is most amazing is the way in which the "rules" of the universe, put to use in this little machine, allow me to execute complicated actions in a mere flash of time. It is no wonder we are enthralled by the possibilities created by our mastery of the natural.

Another nephew of mine works with fibre optics and is devising methods of communication that appear to me to be simple wizardry. His work reminds me that it is now possible for us to communicate with one another more quickly and efficiently than ever before. Yet the implications of this haunt me: we should be better able to understand each other with this possibility, but cultural barriers between countries and belief systems continue to cause disagreements and strife. With so much understanding of the inner dynamics of the created world, the future could be unlimited. It is no wonder that many of us find it easy to suppose that "we can do it ourselves," independent from "old" ideas like "God."

Partners with God have other means of communication. Spiritual connections, even over great distances, are as fast and efficient as fibre optics in providing external links. In fact, connections can be made with people of the past through their writing and art. Creativity connects us, not only with God, but with other human beings. When we are open in spirit, we find a whole reservoir of exciting possibilities. A partner's power is of a different sort than the world seeks to have, demonstrated by his or her unique relationship with God and God's creation.

In his books *Original Blessing* and *A Spirituality Named Compassion*, theologian Matthew Fox helps us to understand this more clearly. He addresses the stress on self-control evident in the community faithstyle. He writes of the difference between climbing a ladder of "goodness" and entering into a dance of life;

i.e., Jacob's ladder versus Sarah's Circle. In the first we ascend to God by good behaviour; in the second, we enter into the life which is available for us as we are. Fox acknowledges the fear that Sarah's Circle might be seen merely as a place of joy and laughter—and creativity.[8] He quotes Meister Eckhart in *Original Blessing*:

> Asceticism is of no great importance. There is a better way to treat your passions than to heap on them practices which so often reveal a great ego and create more instead of less self-consciousness. And that is to put on them a bridle of love. The person who has done this will travel much further than all those the world over practicing mortifications together would ever do.[9]

One reason people find the partnership style so threatening is that partners "seem so free." But let us look at "the bridle of love." A bridle is a steering instrument, assisting one in achieving a goal. It does involve discipline, but it is not "by way of threat, intimidation, or control."[10] Rather it assists discipleship, from which the word discipline is derived. Partnership persons function out of loving and being loved, rather than begging for forgiveness and acceptance. It is like a marriage in which love is so strong that faithfulness need not be forced.

Jesus talked about this kind of deep relationship with God on more than one occasion. "Ye have heard that it hath been said by them of old time" he says of old laws and customs, "but I say unto you" (Matt. 5:21-43, KJV). His new teachings were centred on what a person felt rather than on their outward obedience. Instead of simply obeying the commandment not to kill, he teaches that "whosoever is angry with his brother without a cause shall be in danger of the judgment" (Matt. 5:21-22, KJV). He added an interesting instruction—people were to make peace before they came to worship!

Jesus did not share his people's sense of who was good and who was evil and that God was partial to either group. He says,

> You have heard that it was said, "You shall love your neighbour and hate your enemy." But I say to you, Love your enemies and pray for those who persecute you, so that you may be children of your Father in heaven; for he makes his sun to rise on the evil and on the good, and sends rain on the righteous and the unrighteous (Matt. 5:43-45, NRSV).

For Jesus, the experience of God in nature was related to the spiritual life. He could not have known all the things about the universe that we do, but we can imagine him looking up at the stars and understanding, like Isaiah, that God had put them in place and his loving purpose included all things.

Partners often find that nature nourishes their spiritual life. I live now in a community where there are many bird-watchers. We gleefully welcomed the pair of cardinals when they settled in for the summer. We enjoyed a cedar waxwing that turned up for the first time. I watch the competition for food and the pecking order of the birds at feeders.

One morning I was greeted by the silence of the birds when I awakened—a most unusual occurrence. Then I spotted the reason: a truly beautiful skunk was feeding in my garden. Not until he had taken off did the birds come for their food. Another morning I parted the curtains of my kitchen door and stared straight into the face of a racoon. He looked at me as much as to say, "What are you doing in my world and what, if anything, do you think you can do about my being in yours?" When he saw that I was not going to threaten him, he ambled off to feed contentedly. A chipmunk lives close to my back door. Groundhogs feed all over the lawn. Rabbits frequently come to visit. Since no one in this community has any interest in harming these delightful creatures, they feel safe among us. We put up with missing lettuce and chard in order to enjoy their lives mingling with ours.

When Isaiah writes about the wolf living with the lamb (Isa. 11:6) and Paul writes about how "creation has been groaning in labor pains until now" (Rom. 8:22), they convey some of the Christian hope for the redemption of the whole creation. As the Bible constantly reminds us, God does not see humanity as a separate entity. We belong to the whole. I like the image of "labor pains" for describing the current state of creation. It suggests the unfolding of a meaningful new reality. Granted, it is not fun to live through. There are dangers to be faced in any new situation. However, the hope of new life is real and close and meaningful. Verna McGiffin, with a practical sense of how things come to be, says that we have to begin to train our children for the new tomorrow: "Directed but not dominated, guided but not manipulated, the children of tomorrow ... might develop into responsible adults capable of being stewards of the Earth and guardians of its peoples."[11]

From a very different perspective, male liberationist Sam Keen has made me sharply aware of the way in which our world tends to grab an issue and force a solution. In *Fire in the Belly*, Keen states that men are trained to be warriors. This begins when little boys are not allowed to cry. They are trained to turn off their feelings in order to become more effective fighting machines. Keen believes that this has resulted in the serious wounding of men. It has also resulted in a mechanistic, win or lose, authoritarian style of life, because men have a huge share of power in our world. In fact, men dominate in most fields of endeavour.

Keen feels that men and women need to learn to talk honestly and openly with each other so they can begin to work together. He has a vision of the world: "The great calling of our time that is worthy of men and women is to hold each other within our hearts, and to conspire to create a hearth within the world household." He notes that "these three live or die together: The

Heart. The Hearth. The Earth."[12] He believes that "there is no way for men and women to recover wholeheartedness, to become passionate and truly free, without rediscovering the central importance of the family."[13]

Clearly our universe is in trouble. Partners are persons who are based in deep rather than superficial realities, and who share some of God's pain at the threat of global devastation. They are persons who open themselves to God's way of working, geared more towards McGiffin's and Keen's visions of working with people at their basic need level than with dramatic manipulations or forced obedience to someone else's rules. After all, when God wanted to save people, God sent a tiny, helpless baby into a community in order to help those who knew God grow towards God's Own Self. Partners may very well be the people who live out this vision in our day, but they are not alone. They value the gifts of everyone in our congregations and communities, and they know that it is in sharing that we are able to bring about what is necessary for our continued health together.

To close this section, let us listen again to the voice of Verna Ross McGiffin:

> My spirituality, recognizing the changing concepts of God throughout the ages, had progressed.... I now began to see that my faith could never be static. I wondered if perhaps even the Great Teacher of the Christian faith came, not as the culmination of spirituality, but as a channel through which new spiritual truths might flow."[14]

Those are the words of a partner.

Questions to Consider

1. Can you imagine what it would be like to feel as open as McGiffin to new ways of seeing and being?
2. Does the idea of your being the reflective part of the universe, rather than primarily the caretaker of nature, make you feel like less or more?
3. Do you have trouble being "still" and listening for God's communication with you? Do you believe it can happen? Do you want it?

Chapter Six

Attitudes towards Jesus

Jesus, Friend and Saviour

> *What a friend we have in Jesus*
> *All our sins and griefs to bear!*
>
> Joseph Scriven,
> *The Hymn Book*, #114

This hymn tops the popularity polls of many types of Christian groups. For Christians, it expresses some of the most deeply felt sentiments about Jesus, the man of Nazareth, the Christ, the Saviour of the world. It is not surprising that it was written by a man who had many sorrows. After spending some time in prayer in a friend's home, "God heard and answered, and Joseph Scriven felt the burden miraculously lifted from his heart. In his new-found joy he dashed off a very simple poem...."[1] Since the time when Scriven's friend found the poem and published it, it has been a source of comfort and consolation to countless numbers of Christians.

Close your eyes for a moment now, and think of Jesus. What comes into your mind? What sort of feeling does it bring? There are probably no two people who will have identical experiences during this exercise. Jesus is known about and understood in countless different ways. Community faithstyle persons tend to emphasize Jesus as the lover of children, the one who taught the Golden Rule, and the one who died for us. The harder teachings of Jesus, such as the need to lose your life in order to find it, or to check out where your treasure is, are not that popular. Jesus is sometimes imaged as a loving, indulgent parent who pats one on the head and says, "It's all right now."

Many experience other ways of seeing Jesus. They have struggled with questions such as, "Are you saved?" They have felt pangs of guilt for causing Jesus to suffer and die. They have made a choice at some point in their lives to live in a deliberately Christian way. At the same time, they may often be reluctant to pull together the major teachings of Jesus and apply them to all of life. Security is important in this world, as well as the next—the "Safe in the Arms of Jesus" idea. So is the strengthening of a personal bond, such as in "Take Time to Be Holy" and "Jesus Keep Me Near the Cross." Jesus is a loving friend: "What a Friend We Have in Jesus." Community faithstyle persons know about friends. Jesus often becomes a special friend who can be trusted with any secret. He is the One who understands perfectly. He is always there to help.

To many persons, however, Jesus does not challenge or even question whether he or she is doing right or wrong. If Johnny wants to win a game for his team, he may pray that his star opponent's game will be off. He would not likely want any harm to come to the opposing player in an external sense, but he might if he wanted to impress a new girl friend or receive a pay raise. Jesus' job is to help the one who is praying. How Jesus helps is often seen as magical. One hears fascinating stories about extra-sensory perception, about coincidences that appear to be intentional, about changes that are not easily explained in any other way. Such are the signs of Jesus' friendship and help. They bring great comfort and assurance to many. Some interpret the whole of life in terms of God's goodness. They do not often want to think about these signs in a rational way—they just want to enjoy them and benefit from them.

As an historical person, Jesus is often thought to be "like us," meaning white and English speaking, dark and Spanish, or whatever. He is usually thought to be "meek and mild." Some people are angered by the suggestion that Jesus was, in fact, Jewish, and spoke Aramaic. The possibility of the Holy Family being refugees causes distress, although Matthew's account confirms this (Matt. 2:16-23). The coming of new life and hope out of evil circumstances may be clothed in sentiment. The feeling, though, is a good, warm, reassuring one. He came, the angels sang, the shepherds and wise men worshipped. A new day dawned: "Love Came Down at Christmas."

The Easter story is also softened. Many churches are unaccustomed to celebrating Holy Week. This results in the pleasurable excitement of Palm Sunday and then the glory of Easter morning. The actual events of arrest, whipping and ridicule followed by crucifixion, are glossed over. The events of Holy Thursday are remembered at Communion time in a sentimental way. What the words "Jesus died for us" actually mean seems better left uninvestigated.

Important questions about Christianity are rarely asked. For example: Is Jesus really the Son of God? If so, how? The Virgin Birth story suggests that one-half of Jesus' genetic inheritance is of God. How could this be? Is this the same God who "walked in the garden in the cool of the day?" (Gen. 3:8). Is God a man? The Shorter Catechism states that we cannot see God because "God is a Spirit and has not a body as we have." Does this not contradict the traditional view of the Bible, that God *does* have a body? Could a spirit beget a child? This is very difficult ground for community faithstyle persons who think in a concrete way. In a recent debate about inclusive language at a National

Methodist Conference in the United States, one man confi-
dently told a television reporter that "everybody *knows* God is a
man."

Knowing the background of the Bible is helpful. The Greek
religions, for example, have many human-god birth stories. In
the days when the Gospels were being written, this would not
have seemed strange. For people who take the Bible literally,
however, this poses a real problem. If the Bible cannot be in error
in any detail, the Spirit that came upon Mary had to have
physical properties—the ability to impregnate a woman. Is the
Catechism wrong? It is a lot easier for people to think about this
question than whether Jesus is really the Son of God. They can
usually find like-minded people who also wonder about these
things. They may be able to accept that the writers of the Bible
used stories to express truth, as Jesus often did. They may write
a poem, as did the prophets, using word pictures like a valley of
dry bones coming to life (Ezek. 37:1-14). Or they may use a
common idea to explain something new—like Paul pointing out
to the Athenians that they have a statue to an unknown god.
"That's the one," Paul says, "I've come to talk about." He
connects with their life experience (Acts 17:23).

What is the point that the writers of the Virgin Birth story are
trying to make? That people experienced the Jewish God in
Jesus. Just that. He was not like others who spoke about God. He
spoke with authority (Mark 1:22). He did not live like other
religious leaders. He lived in communion with God throughout
his life, not just in times and ways prescribed by The Law (Mark
12:38-40; Luke 6:12). What phrase might carry some of that
meaning? Son of God, surely. But if "son" implies a physical
relationship, then why use a Virgin Birth story in the first place?
Because people would understand it. They did, of course, then,
but now people are confused. Now it is a problem. We want to
reduce truth to strictly physical facts. We forget, sometimes, that
the Bible is really about the meaning of our lives in relation to

the life and will of our Creator. The Bible is not a science textbook.

A son, in any case, may be like his father or not. The truth the Bible is telling us is that Jesus revealed God—as much as any human being can. He was the fulfilment of all the things promised by the prophets. Jews have never accepted that, but Christians have. He is the Messiah (the Anointed One), the Christ. Jews believe that he was a prophet, but they still expect their Messiah.

The proof of Jesus' specialness to Christians is the resurrection. The Jews thought he was effectively destroyed. Surprise! On Sunday morning the stone is rolled back. He is gone. He said he would do it and he did. Jesus is alive again. Now here surely is proof for community faithstyle persons, but no, here again we are hung up on a physical point. Since we have to deal with the physical reality of conception, we have to deal with the physical reality of a dead body. What happened to it? The Jews claimed it was stolen in spite of the guards they placed at the tomb (Matt. 28:11-15). The Christians saw Jesus in a special form (which could, for example, come through closed doors [John 20:26]) several times in the next forty days. Paul tells us in I Corinthians 15:3-7 that Jesus appeared to Peter and then to the twelve apostles. "Then he appeared to more than five hundred of his followers at once, most of whom are still alive, although some have died. Then he appeared to James and afterward to all the apostles." There are still witnesses alive at the time of writing!

We know now that an experience called "incorporation" can happen after the death of a loved one. We "see" them whole and seemingly real. Jesus, however, ate with the disciples (Luke 24:42-43). He must have had a special form. Community faithstyle persons have an answer: "With God all things are possible." There is, however, another mystery. What became of the physical body when it left the tomb? How was it unwrapped? Where did it go? To Jews, the body and the spirit are one reality. It is not satisfactory to say that the spirit left the body, as the Greeks would say, and that the body no longer mattered. Jesus had a body when he appeared to Mary and the others—not a regular body, but a body. Paul helps us comprehend this mystery in I Corinthians 15:35-50, when he writes of the resurrection body.

We may be reminded, however, that we still have flesh and bones in a tomb. They disappeared, although we may never know how. It is an important reminder that there are mysteries in our Christian faith. We can only go so far in understanding, and then no farther; we have to leave the rest to God. What we do know is what resulted. People came to know the living Jesus, not as a physical oddity, but as a spiritual guide and healer. At Pentecost, the Holy Spirit he had promised came in power (Acts 2). This Spirit, mentioned in the Old Testament, was specifically linked to the man Jesus. People came to realize that God, Jesus, and the Holy Spirit are one. We can pray to any or all of them and reach the same source of help.

Christianity grew and spread throughout the Mediterranean world by the time the New Testament was completed. Later it spread throughout the whole world. The wisdom of Gamaliel was thus proven. The disciples had been called before the Jewish Council. Gamaliel had said, "If what they have planned and done is of human origin it will disappear, but if it comes from God, you cannot possibly defeat them. You could find yourselves fighting against God!" (Acts 5:38-39, TEV).

We can know the reality of God in Jesus and the Holy Spirit. Community faithstyle persons do not often feel that they need theological "proofs." They simply believe. Their ability to accept mystery is probably larger than that of most people who study, think, and write about these things. Their faith may, in fact, be greater. Their Jesus may, indeed, be their friend through good times and bad. Those who pass superficial judgement on the community faithstyle position would do well to seriously consider the positive aspects of it with regard to Jesus.

Questions to Consider

1. Who is Jesus to you?
2. Is the Virgin Birth something we have to accept as it is written in Matthew and Luke?
3. What about the resurrection would be most satisfying for you to know? Why?
4. What would life be like if Jesus had not come?

Searching for the Truth of the Gospel

*If the spirit of [humans beings] and the spirit of God
inhabit the same world, that fact is more important
than the theological relation between them.*

Northrop Frye,
The Double Vision, 84

Northrop Frye, one of Canada's most famous scholars, was also a minister of The United Church of Canada. I remember when he pronounced the benediction at the end of Senate meetings while serving as Chancellor of Victoria University in Toronto. It was an awesome experience to hear the familiar words, spoken with such clear spiritual feeling, from a man who lived intellectually in such a rarefied atmosphere.

In *The Double Vision*, Frye addresses some of the more perplexing religious questions in today's world. He says, for example, that

> there is no certainty in faith to begin with: we are free to deny the reality of the spiritual challenge of the New Testament, and if we accept it, we accept it tentatively, taking a risk. The certainty comes later, and very gradually, with the growing sense in our own experience that the vision really does have the power that it claims to have.[2]

However, he later adds:

> What "the" truth is, is not available to human beings in spiritual matters: the goal of our spiritual life is God, who is a spiritual Other, not a spiritual object, much less a conceptual object. That is why the Gospels keep reminding us how many listen and how few hear: truths of the gospel kind cannot be demonstrated except through personal example.[3]

To some searchers, this will not be "good news." The effort to understand with the mind is often their most compelling motive. It is certainly possible to accumulate all kinds of facts, to do a comparative analysis of Christianity and other religions, and to study the various creeds of the different denominations. It is even possible, if one is so inclined, to do research on the effects of religion. An example of that was published in *Newsweek* and reprinted in *Reader's Digest*, with the title, "Why People Pray." The study, done by the National Opinion Research Centre at the University of Chicago, concluded that most people pray and that prayer is "good for you." The article points out that "the first big step is to cease talking *to* God and start listening *for* God. And that requires silence, a nearly forgotten dimension of modern life."[4] It is relationship that counts!

And so we have Jesus among us, human like us, born of a woman, needing to eat, sleep, and rest. In order to be a Christian, one must believe in Jesus. He was a man born in a little occupied country in the days of the Roman Empire, but that is not all that he was. Jesus came to a people who were expecting a Messiah— an "Anointed One"—to deliver them from their oppression and give them power and glory instead. The world was to be ruled from Jerusalem. The Romans, naturally, did not take kindly to this dream of the Jews. Hence, Jesus was suspected of being a troublemaker as soon as he demonstrated his extraordinary power for attracting crowds, for healing, and for provoking thought.

To believe that Jesus is "the Christ" (which is the Greek translation of the Hebrew word "Messiah") is another matter. It means that one has accepted Jesus as a special communicator of God. It is a matter of faith, not simply an acceptance of something in history. Jesus is still a man but he also shares in the nature of God. I find it useful to think that when one comes into God's presence, with or through Christ, there is no sense of difference between them. "The Father and I are one," said Jesus

(John 10:30). This is the experience of faith. This cannot easily be explained, but it is reality for a Christian—the same reality that has made Christianity, in fact, a major world religion.

We have many ways of approaching the evidence of how this came to be. Matthew and Luke give us miraculous birth stories in the style of their times. Mark dwells on Jesus' many miracles. John is a philosopher-theologian. Therefore, tradition, historical events, and scholarly thinking are all used to present something of what Jesus was found to be. Yet none of these completes the picture. It is when we read Acts (2:14-42) and find the newly brave Peter preaching on Pentecost—even though he knew that he might be killed for it—that we realize we have moved into a new day. A new energy has been released into the world. God's Grace has become obvious to more people as the result of Jesus' life, death, and resurrection. Some people get hung up on the physical details, but none of them are as important as this fact: God has been revealed in a wonderfully new and effective way.

Scholars love big words and precise definitions. They have developed concepts like reconciliation, atonement, and propitiatory "satisfaction" to explain what Jesus did for us. We have a wide range of images from which to draw our conclusions. The satisfaction theory is related to "the blood of the Lamb" and to the Agnus Dei, which is often used in services: "O Lamb of God, who takest away the sin of the world, have mercy upon us." This idea is based on the cultic sacrifices of animals in the temple. Reconciliation refers to our being estranged from God through Adam's and our own sin. It means becoming friends again— "coming home" as one hymn puts it—by accepting Jesus Christ's gift of giving his life for us. Atonement is my favourite: at-one-ment. Jesus makes us one with the Spirit of God, not through a legal requirement or a reckoning of our sins, but through an outpouring of unconditional love.

Whether or not Jesus is central in our theology is hotly debated in some churches today. Many are trying to bring about a balance in our view of the Trinity. It has seemed to be neglected, at times, in favour of what might be called a cozy view of Jesus and his chosen few. There are radical fundamentalists, not only in Christianity, but in the world at large. Perhaps the stress of these times has created more of a need for "certainties" and enforced rules. This can create a painful difference in the way we relate to others. Searchers may be "turned off" by all the fighting.

The idea of the "chosen people" is a very old one. It turns up very dramatically in the stories of the Exodus from Egypt and the conquering of Canaan. This Jewish idea became part of the Christian belief system partly because Jesus said, "No one comes to the Father except through me" (John 14:6, *NIV*). It is part of his last conversation with the disciples. I personally believe that he meant to put the emphasis on the "father" part of this statement. He constantly talked with God and called God "Abba" (Daddy). This was a radically new way of communicating with the One Holy God of Israel. He seems to me to be saying that if anyone wishes to know God as a loving father, he is the one who can help with that.

In my opinion, Jesus would not have meant that there is no other way to get to God. Clearly, he did not behave like a proud member of an exclusive club; he denounced the scribes and the Pharisees precisely for that. He behaved like one of God's people—honouring family traditions, but not bound by them, because his own relationship with God taught him new things. Since Jesus identified himself with Isaiah's prophecy at the very beginning of his ministry, according to Luke (4:16-19), he was conscious of the need for good news for the needy, and believed God's Spirit was upon him. Isaiah had a clear sense of God being concerned for all people. We have no reason to believe that Jesus felt differently.

I would love to have Jesus here among us in person. I do not pretend, however, that he would be easier to live with now than he was in the first century. He provokes us into thinking and forces us to face the reality of some of the things we do, but he also sees who we are capable of becoming. He would not want us to make him into a giant cradle to rock us to sleep. He keeps saying, in effect, "There is work to be done, the good news has to be lived. What are you willing to do about it? The needs are all around you. Come with me. I need you!"

This is all part of the New Testament truth to which Frye referred. Throughout the centuries, theologians have "explained" all kinds of things about Jesus. However, when you come right down to it, you have to decide for yourself whether or not Jesus is a person to follow. Searchers may spend years studying all the evidence of The Jesus Seminar—which seeks to find the "real" words of Jesus in the Gospel records—and still never reach a conclusion unless they are open to the Spirit. Frye reminds us that searching may be deeply satisfying in many ways, and theology may be a most interesting study, but "when the chips are down," we need basics, and the basic thing is that God is with us. In Jesus, we meet God, or we do not. Jesus, as a man, is an interesting prophet of the first century. Jesus as Man-God, or God-Man, leads us to the heart of our Creator God. The records about him lead us to the kind of life we were designed to live. To searchers, the key is found when they feel his Spirit in their hearts.

Questions to Consider

1. Would Jesus have been more or less important if he had lived out a normal life span? Why?
2. Does it make sense to say that a person needs to meet an underlying "spirit" to believe someone is who they claim to be?
3. Does it really matter if each word in the Bible is true, at least in some sense, if not literally? Does it change Jesus?
4. Would you like to have Jesus as a neighbour? Why?

Experiencing Jesus in Us and the World

Bind yourself to Jesus, therefore, in faith and love, so that belonging to him you may share all he has and enter the fellowship of those who love him.

Anonymous,
The Cloud of Unknowing, 51

Down through the centuries there have been people who dedicated their whole lives to prayer and contemplation. *The Cloud of Unknowing* was written primarily for these groups. Nevertheless, it gives guidance to anyone interested in deepening their spiritual life. One of my favourite comments is: "When [contemplative work] is genuine it is simply a spontaneous desire springing suddenly toward God like spark from a fire."[5] Partners know how that feels. There is something inherently mysterious and wonder-filled in this experience.

Partners have generally been through both community and searcher styles, but not always! It is important to realize that many people come to the partnership faithstyle without a classical Christian background. They may "discover" God in nature, at a meeting or retreat, by reading or talking with others who may or may not be Christian. In such circumstances, Jesus may be either missing or over-emphasized, depending on the source of discovery. The motivation for practicing meditation, for example, may be a desire for self-improvement or the solution to a problem. If clergy or other Christians want to be of help to these persons, they need to listen carefully and find out where the person *is* before they even think of making suggestions. If the person is seeking God in Christianity, they may need background information. This would include an introduction to the Bible and a summary of the Judeo-Christian family story. It would also include some discussion about what the Judeo-Christian God is likely to do—or not to do—when people attempt to make connections. As Jesus' life story makes abundantly clear, there is no guarantee of happiness. We do have, however, a genuine companion to share the road with us.

Many community faithstyle persons have rich devotional lives, often centred on Jesus. They may have regular Quiet Times, shared Bible study, retreats, and so on. Spiritual growth may be a priority in their lives. As Lawrence LeShan notes in *How to Meditate*, things may happen that cannot happen during the normal state of consciousness (such as telepathy) and "many people ... get so interested in them and excited about their occurrence that they lose all their orientation to the real goals of meditation. They become more concerned with the paranormal than with their own development.... Unless this orientation is given up, further development is very unlikely."[6] We need to remember, however, that some community faithstyle persons have a partnership style devotional life while participating in the outward practices of their community.

The key difference between the two styles is the openness of the partnership faithstyle. Our fourteenth-century anonymous author wrote of belonging to Jesus and sharing "all he has." This is almost heretical to community faithstyle persons who, on the one hand, have a sense of Jesus' closeness, but feel on the other that he is a crowned figure in heaven. Some hymns that proclaim this are, "Rejoice, The Lord is King"; "All Hail the Power of Jesus' Name"; and "Thine is the Glory." Here the spiritual bond is based on Jesus graciously reaching out to the person. In comparison, the partner's spiritual bond is based on entering a union of shared reality, as Jesus foretold: "On that day you will know that I am in my Father, and you in me, and I in you" (John 14:20, NRSV).

Community faithstyle persons often say, "Jesus died for me." As fundamental as Jesus' death may be, this saving event still feels distant to them, no matter how well understood it is. The God-Jesus-believer oneness of the partnership style means that, not only does the partner feel what it is like for Jesus to die, but that God does too. Therefore, God is capable of feeling our pain *with us*. God shares in the resurrection and in our lives, as we move through and away from pain. Jesus brings God into the centre of our lives if we allow it. He helps us to know "in our bones" how God and human beings are intimately related. This means, among other things, that partners are not "only on Sunday" Christians. They seek to be with Jesus and God as often as possible. St. Teresa of Avila expressed it this way:

> Take pleasure in remaining in His society: do not lose such precious time, for this hour is of the utmost value to the soul, and the good Jesus desires you to spend it with Him…. He will not show Himself openly or reveal His glories or bestow His treasures, save on souls who prove that they ardently desire Him, for these are His real friends.[7]

Notice the difference between this idea of friendship and the one found in "What a Friend We Have in Jesus."

Jesus is often left out or put aside in current thinking within mainline churches. It is almost as if John's message about Jesus and God and believer together forming one has been missed in some cases. However, there is another factor that has to do with the human relationship to the whole of creation. In the "peak experience" of which psychologist Abraham Maslow writes, in the "God-grounded self" referred to by James Fowler, and in the "participants in grace" experience that theologian Douglas John Hall describes, there is a sense of being one with creation that is uncharacteristic of traditional Christian thought.

Maslow writes as a psychologist and sees Jesus as the founder of a great world religion. Fowler sees the God-grounded self as the highest stage of faith development. Hall calls people to participate in Christ's sufferings and quotes Paul: "Do you not know that all of us who have been baptized into Christ Jesus were baptized into his death? We were buried therefore with him by baptism into death, so that as Christ was raised from the dead by the glory of the Father, we too might walk in newness of life (Rom.6:3,4)."[8] This attitude was real to the early Christians, but has gradually been lost. However, if we take seriously what Jesus said about being "in my Father, and you in me, and I in you," we are participants in, not recipients of, the work of Jesus.

It is interesting that Fowler and Hall insist that we as Christians have to identify ourselves with the work of redemption in the world now. Fowler states that faith development is not a goal in itself. Rather it is "a byproduct of our work and that of the spirit of God as we try to be faithfully responsive to the call of God to partnership." It works "toward God's goal of a universal commonwealth of love and justice."[9] Hall states that

> what must not be upheld ... is the kind of spectator spirituality which, having taken to itself in some domesticated form 'the benefits of *his* passion,' is itself able to exist in a suffering world without either passion or compassion.... [The Christian faith] will be assessed finally, not on the basis of the adequacy or inadequacy of its theology, but, like all things else, by its fruits, that is, on the basis of the church's deportment of *itself* in a suffering world.[10]

The issue, clearly, is one of context. If we think of Jesus as *our* Saviour and Christianity as the only worthy religion, we have a limited view of what we are to be about. *The Hymn Book* contains a stunning number of hymns that emphasize power and glory. We have a lot of warlike ideas as well as a heavenly vision of triumph. In the partner's spiritual experience of oneness with God, Christ, the Spirit, and the created universe, there is no room for this limited view. This does not mean that true partners de-emphasize the importance of Jesus. Rather, it means that partners want to get to work on what Jesus was, and is, working on—they want to participate with him in what needs to be done for the good of the whole world.

It is important here to note the difference between the idea of "winning" by destroying your "enemies" and the idea of working collaboratively with human needs to bring about benefit for all. Feminists have made us sharply aware of the harsh, controlling, combative stance of much Christian thinking. They suggest that we move towards a style that encourages growth and development within us, so that we may operate from a base of love for all and concern for justice for everyone. Yet both of these styles need to be examined in the light of the cross.

Jesus did not organize an army or even take part in anti-Roman raids, so far as we know, but neither was he the "Gentle Jesus, meek and mild" of the children's hymn. He had a clear sense of divine purpose and was not distracted from it. That purpose was to introduce a new spiritual element into his people's traditional faith—the Law was to be internalized (written on people's hearts), and the people were to operate out of their spiritual life, rather than from a book of rules. It was a new style of faith, but it did not destroy the old; it fulfilled it (Matt. 5). Not everyone wanted it, to put it mildly, but that did not deter him. He believed in it so strongly that he was willing to die for it, and through that death, he proclaimed for all time that apparent weakness may be the greatest strength. He did this only after many, many hours of being with God in prayer, allowing the reality of the Spirit to guide him. In Gethsemane we see how hard the whole thing was for him, but he did not turn back. He did, indeed, "die for us."

What we think of Jesus is the essential core of our Christian faith. The old images and symbols still have significance for me, but I have also caught the vision of some of the new images and symbols that prompted Jesus and countless others to think in larger terms. I am deeply conscious of the way in which our world is changing, and I do not think that any factor, such as race, skin colour, or traditional faith, makes any people the most important in the world. Nevertheless, we Christians are a people who have received a great treasure in the Judeo-Christian story of faith as it develops through the centuries. We have a unique way of seeing God's loving purpose as it is worked out on a large scale, over a long time, using the gifts of the people of each age. If we catch some of Jesus' own vision, it helps us enormously.

Finally, some words from Teilhard de Chardin. He wrote: "Love is the only force that can make things one without destroying them."[11] The love of Jesus is one of the greatest forces ever experienced in this world.

Questions to Consider

1. Are you satisfied with your present spiritual life?
2. Meditation has to be continued to be worthwhile. Could you manage the time and effort for it in your life?
3. Does the idea of sharing in Jesus' life and purpose now appeal to you? Make you afraid? Reluctant?
4. Might it be easier just to be a receiver than to be both a receiver and a partner with Jesus? What would you miss?

Chapter Seven

Opinions of The Bible

God's Living Word

> O Christ the Word incarnate,
> O Wisdom from on high,
> O Truth unchanged, unchanging,
> O Light of our dark sky:
> we praise you for the radiance
> that from the hallowed page
> a lantern to our footsteps,
> shines on from age to age.
>
> William W. How,
> *Songs for a Gospel People*, #22[1]

There is probably nothing more central or debated in the Christian belief system than the authority of the Bible. Churches have repeatedly been divided over either the meaning of one particular biblical statement or the correct attitude towards it. Credal statements of one historical period have been vigorously challenged in another. The Reformation was based on radically different interpretations of the meaning of the Bible's statements about faith and the role of the laity from the Roman Catholic Church of the sixteenth century.

The United Church of Canada has a Basis of Union statement, which, for some people, is absolutely vital to faith. It says that the Bible *is* the Word of God. When a new United Church Statement of Faith was written in 1940, the Bible was seen as "the true witness to God's Word and the sure guide to Christian faith and conduct."[2] This shift has had many practical consequences. The most recent and most publicized were the heated debates concerning the ordination of gays and lesbians. If every single word of the Bible is literally true, any practice of homosexuality is forbidden. If the expressed intent of the 1940 Statement of Faith is valid, then the Holy Scriptures contain, not only records of historical events, but more important, various interpretations of God's witness throughout history.

R. Theodore Lutz, United Church minister and Old Testament scholar, states that there are four main ways of recognizing the authority of the Bible:

1. *Inerrancy*: God is the ultimate author; therefore, there can be no error in the Bible. For example, Genesis 1-11 records eternal scientific and historical truth. People who believe this have enormous trouble with translations. They tend to resist reading or listening to any version but that of King James, which was originally translated in 1611. Textual problems raised by the modern discovery of conflicting ancient manuscripts or factual contradictions within the text itself are explained away or simply ignored. The Bible is holy. To some it is almost magical. Certainly it is the centre of faith, never to be questioned. All the books within it are believed to be equally valuable as guides to Christian conduct.

2. *Infallibility*: In this belief system it is acknowledged that the Bible is primarily about faith and our knowledge of God, not

about science and history. Those persons who have chosen this position maintain that, on matters of faith and theology, the Bible cannot be wrong. The problem of the nature of inspiration is subsequently raised. How do we then determine which passages are actually inspired by God and which are not?

3. A third theory is that "inspiration is to be seen operating on the level of ideas" and not in the actual words. People relate to events in a variety of ways: i.e., in order to tell the Christmas story, Matthew gives chronological details in recounting Jesus' genealogy, while John writes a hymn. Both are communicating to us that God was in Jesus. The theological point is the same. Community faithstyle persons, however, which the early Christians generally were, may prefer the "facts" in Matthew's story to the "philosophy" of John. It is the difference between concrete reality and the world of ideas. The problem, again, is knowing what the particular writer meant and how readers interpret the words. Many battles have been fought over the meaning of some scriptural passages.

4. *God inspired the community that received and preserved the words of individual writers.* Different circumstances and peoples were transformed by their community's understanding of the messages and what they did about them. The creation of the Bible itself is the result of inspiration. Jesus clearly believed that additions could be made. In Matthew 13:52, he states: Every teacher of the law who has been instructed about the kingdom of heaven is like the owner of a house who brings out of his storeroom new treasures as well as old (*NIV*). Jesus did not reject the Law of his Jewish community but simply enlarged the understanding of it.

In this fourth view, according to Lutz, *the Church today is given authority to make new rules, under inspiration, which are consistent with tradition.* The Church defined the canon of scripture as we have it. It recognized the authority in the books included. This authority is based on its power to change people and to make a vital connection with God, but it is not the only way to connect with God. Lutz believes that the Church, functioning as the Church, has the authority to reach decisions not found in the Bible. God is still working through individuals and communities. Inspiration goes on. However, the word of people who claim to be inspired has to be tested against the traditions in the Bible. If someone comes in with a gun and says, "God told me to shoot all preachers," we would be highly suspicious of this person's received "inspiration." In all ages, God has chosen witnesses, and their messages have enabled faith communities to live and grow. What is often overlooked is the fact that biblical scholars use modern techniques for studying ancient manuscripts and languages *in order to get closer to the original meaning.*

"The authority of the Bible lies in the authenticity of the message it brings," writes Lutz. We are people of the New Covenant written on our hearts (Jer. 31:33). Christ himself is the instrument of change, not the Law. By identifying with Christ we become part of the Christian community—part of the ongoing witness to the world of God's care. Consequently, "the authority of the Bible lies in its power to shape human existence."[3]

It is a long way from the beginning of the first main way of recognizing the authority of the Bible to the end of the fourth. The inerrancy theory makes God the One Who Acts—God gives, inspires, and works through the words of the Bible. In the other theories, God also acts, but the collective human experience is emphasized. Thus, people are more than receptacles of Gods revelations; they are involved in discerning what God has done, is doing, or wants to do. The meanings themselves are important and are shaped by both God and persons of faith.

Community faithstyle persons generally view the Bible as literally true—but not always! Parts that are difficult are often ignored. The Ten Commandments, the Golden Rule, and other chosen parts form a kind of sub-text, which, in reality, is the accepted guide for many parishioners. However, important differences are notable through particular generations. Senior Christians have often studied the Bible, both privately and in groups, and may know it well. Middle-aged persons may be a part of that tradition or only interested in reading selected parts. Younger adults often have a disturbing lack of biblical knowledge—disturbing because many have come through Sunday school classes, at least up to their teen years. The frequent lack of overall attention to how God and people work together is strange. Some of the stories of the Bible are remembered, but not their point. This is a major problem in our churches.

Community faithstyle persons of the "old school" tend to base their faith more on "getting to heaven" than on finding meaning in this world. Self-sacrifice, for example, is thought to be "good" because it strengthens the soul and prepares it for the next life. To the extent that it has become a value in itself, younger generations are often harshly judged for not sacrificing more of themselves. The "me generation" has no understanding of, or desire to live by, such a view, as it simply makes no sense to them. In order to have meaning for younger people, self-sacrifice has to be rooted in the whole life and teaching of Jesus. It is unreasonable to expect people of today to pick up and live by the values of the past without a firm understanding of their roots. To try to instil old and misunderstood values in younger generations is to ask for trouble. This is, perhaps, the most important lesson community faithstyle persons need to learn. The Bible as authority, however, can be very clear about the consequences of non-obedience. It is not surprising that older persons frequently agonize over the ways of "young people." Older believers have a two-edged concern—what it means in the present and what it may mean in the future. Reunion with loved ones in heaven is a precious and lively hope for many of them.

Among the present concerns of many families are instances of adultery (seventh Commandment broken—Ex. 20:14) and fornication (for example, Matt. 15:19, *NRSV*, lists fornication with evil intentions, murder, adultery, theft, false witness, slander) and remarriage, though Jesus disapproves (in Matthew 19:9: "Whoever divorces his wife, except for unchastity, and marries another, commits adultery."). Younger people often do not understand the depth of the problem. Meanwhile, fear of the wrath of God can be devastating, not to mention fear of the community's anger towards those who "err." Community faithstyle persons place a high value on self-control and on "making the best of it." If you make a mistake, you pay for it. You take your punishment, which may mean being ostracized. What's right is right, some may say, to further justify their condemnation of sexual sinners.

Marriage is not to be taken lightly but "reverently, discreetly, soberly and in the fear of God" as the 1950 United Church of Canada marriage service puts it. The reality, however, is that the Bible came from a very different time and place. The culture that produced its values was entirely different from ours. It was even more patriarchal—women belonged to men, much like a piece of land or equipment. They were expected to be virgins until betrothed, and they were to be faithful for the duration of their lives. In return, men were to provide for them and treat them well. Throughout the Bible, men were permitted to have more than one wife. In one of the latest books, Timothy explicitly directs that bishops have to be the husband of one wife (I Tim. 3:12). The Bible simply has no understanding of modern women, although women like Priscilla and Lydia, who worked with St. Paul, come close. The dire warnings about women are all aimed at either prostitutes or adulteresses. They were seen as a source of evil by many biblical writers. Prostitutes were frequently temple prostitutes—both male and female—meaning they participated in some pagan form of cultic worship referred to in both the Old and New Testaments.

Moses had given men the right to divorce women by the simple method of writing three times on a strip of paper, "I divorce you." The woman then had to leave (without her children, if the husband so chose) and go to her nearest male relative. Jesus saw clearly how vulnerable women were in this system and how hurt they could be. Therefore, he forbade divorce *under those circumstances.* We can only guess what Jesus would say today. He said that adultery is a sin but he stopped the legal stoning of a woman "caught in the very act." He told her, "Do not sin again" (John 8:3-11, *NRSV*). Jesus, however, was fully aware of how actions begin in our minds and feelings (in Matt. 15:19, he states, "Out of the heart come evil intentions," *NRSV*). This view was quite different from that of the religious authorities at that time. Obeying the Law in itself was what was required.

Paul consistently includes fornication and adultery in the lists of sins in his letters. We need to remember that he was not working in a Jewish environment, although he was raised a strict Jew. On one level, Greek and Roman societies were very similar to our own. Paul saw the need to choose which way one would live—according to "human nature," or by the "spiritual nature" that Christ gives (Gal. 5:16-26). He saw people become "new creatures in Christ Jesus" and saw how they were empowered to be quite different. They were not only able to obey the outward forms demanded of them, but were capable of being deeply satisfied and at peace with God in their daily lives. There is a world of difference between the experience of God among the Jewish people of the Old Testament and the reality of God as experienced by Jesus and his followers.

The Bible is a record of a long and complicated journey of understanding. The Jews interpreted their history in terms of what they believed God was doing among them. When bad things happened, they believed that God was punishing them.

For Jesus, however, God was quite different—God works for our good and forgives our sins. God welcomes us as beloved children. The Bible gives us countless pictures of God, and we need to keep them all in mind in order to have a balanced view. Yet, for Christians, Jesus is the best revelation of God's nature. Jesus is neither as soft as we sometimes would like, nor as hard as we sometimes fear. His words about love are rooted in reality and his gift to us radically changes our lives. The Word of God is a Word of love and power together—a Living Word!

Questions to consider

1. What do you think of the Bible?
2. If God is communicating with us through the Bible, could the message be somehow clearer?
3. Do you receive inspiration and strength from reading or remembering the Bible?
4. What are your favourite parts or ideas in the Bible?

Looking for Evidence

One by one, the illusions I had had of the God of the Old Testament fell away as I realized that the Bible had been written, not by a single author, but by many. These writers would naturally speak from their own viewpoints, prejudices and hopes. Consequently, they would portray various and changing concepts of the nature of God. I could recognize that their writings would reflect the level of knowledge of the people of the times in which they lived.

Verna Ross McGiffin,
In Search of Wisdom, 38

In the quote above, McGiffin has touched on what is common to all searchers; i.e., that the Bible must become an historical book, subject to the investigations of all such books, if it is to be understood by someone seeking the truth for themselves and this age. The Bible records an unfolding story of the communications between God and human beings. Searchers need to follow the path of God's increasing revelation of God's Own Self. The Bible becomes more significant as the search goes on, but this first step cannot be omitted.

The Bible consists of ancient stories passed on from generation to generation. These stories were collected and edited only when writing on papyrus (a type of reed) became possible. The only stories that lasted beyond the oral form are those that carried an important meaning for an audience. They had to somehow "come alive" in the thoughts and/or feelings of those who listened. That capacity to come alive is the central quality of myth. It shows that the meaning of the story is true to the people's experience, even if the event related was not an historical fact. The most significant myth for searchers of our day is the story of Adam and Eve, because it touches the base of our beliefs about creation, sexual roles, and sin.

It may not be easy for searchers to accept the mythic nature of the story of Adam and Eve. It upsets all the pre-conceived ideas many people have about a supernatural series of events that gave human beings the responsibility for exercising proper "dominion over the fish of the sea, and over the fowl of the air, and over every living thing that moveth upon the earth" (Gen. 1:28, *KJV*). The meaning of that particular statement is still being debated as we are beginning to think more and more about our role in caring for the planet Earth. This was not questioned in the past—it was understood to mean that we had the right to use nature just as we pleased in order to meet our needs.

Actually, the first part of Genesis 1:28 carries a slightly different message. In the *KJV*, it reads: "And God blessed them, and God said unto them, Be fruitful, and multiply, and replenish the earth, and subdue it." Many of the ancient creation myths, from places such as Canaan or Babylonia, tell of creation forming from struggle. They portray a divine struggle with waters and a climactic victory over chaos of the kind found in the biblical poetry of Psalm 29.

A related element in the Bible, which is not commonly cited, is that of wisdom. According to *Harper's Bible Dictionary*, the old tradition that "divine Wisdom was the agent of creation ... appears both in the Old Testament (e.g. Prov. 8:25-27) and in apocryphal writings (e.g. Wisdom of Solomon 7:24-25; Ecclus. 24:3, 9)."[4] In *The Jerusalem Bible*, Proverbs 8:22-31 reads:

Yahweh [God] created me when his purpose first unfolded,
before the oldest of his works.
From everlasting I was firmly set,
from the beginning, before earth came into being.
The deep was not, when I was born,
there were no springs to gush with water.

Before the mountains were settled,
before the hills, I came to birth;
before he made the earth, the countryside,
or the first grains of the world's dust.
When he fixed the heavens firm, I was there,
when he drew a ring on the surface of the deep,
when he thickened the clouds above,
when he fixed fast the springs of the deep,
when he assigned the sea its boundaries
—and the waters will not invade the shore—
when he laid down the foundation of the earth,
I was by his side, a master craftsman,
delighting him day after day,
ever at play in his presence,
at play everywhere in his world,
delighting to be with the sons of men.

This is a very different picture of creation. Wisdom, which is used in the feminine gender, is usually presented in the Bible as wise advice on how to live life. Proverbs, Job, and Ecclesiastes are the three books of Wisdom in Protestant Bibles. They specialize in good advice. I have quoted from the Biblical Wisdom literature to illustrate how many things in the Bible can be obscured by some of the prevalent assumptions about scripture. For example, we never heard of play and delight at the creation of the world in my Sunday school!

Searchers tend to want to read and study, but they also need discussion with others as they go along. They may be enthusiastic about different things at various points in their search. I remember when an article about the Dead Sea Scrolls (ancient manuscripts of the Bible) was published in a mass circulation newspaper. A store keeper rather excitedly told me that Jesus had been an Essene who decided not to stay with the community in the desert but decided instead "to share the news with others about what life could be." Having seen the site of the Essene community near the Dead Sea, I can imagine such a decision! I have since realized, however, that we do not know what Jesus was doing in those silent years before he began to travel about, preaching, teaching, and healing. We know that he was developing a close relationship with God, so close that he did not address God with the formal "Father" that we use.

Searchers look for facts and may be frustrated that no video camera was available to provide us with a retrospective of Jesus' life. They may read various interpretations of it—from the devotional account of Herbert O. Driscoll to the psychiatric account of Albert Schweitzer to the fact-based imaginative narrative of Anthony Burgess.[5] They may listen to the rock musical *Jesus Christ, Superstar* and see the modern film *Jesus of Montreal*. They may talk to agnostics and people of other faiths. This phenomenon is similar to looking at a crystal in various shades of light. Turning it about will produce very different effects but the base reality does not change. It is how we perceive it that changes. The life of Jesus will always have an element of mystery about it.

The most important part of the search, however, is not the investigation itself. Rather, it relates to the question: Does this faith work? Everyone who claims to be a Christian and becomes involved with searchers is liable to be judged—and may arouse the suspicions of those community faithstyle persons surrounding them. Christianity does promise a great deal. If one claims to have new life in Christ as promised in the Bible, it is characteristic for a searcher to say, "Show me." This can easily put others off, particularly those of the community faithstyle. They may find themselves feeling angry, defensive, or challenged to live more consistently according to what they say they believe. We are most helpful to searchers when we are honest. The Bible does say that Jesus gives peace, yet many of us are not at peace and certainly the world is not. In John 14, Jesus is not talking to the world, but to his disciples. He knows that he is going to be killed. He tells them that the Holy Spirit, the Comforter (*KJV*), the Advocate (*NRSV*), will come to help them. They will not be alone. Countless people through the ages have found that this comfort and help are real. Searchers need to hear such reassurance.

Sometimes, if we are honest, we as Christians will need to admit that we're having a rough time. We don't help anybody, least of all ourselves, if we deny it. The Bible gives us evidence that God accepts our rage as well as our love. Consider Lamentations 3:43: "You [God] have wrapped yourself with anger and pursued us, killing without pity; you have wrapped yourself with a cloud so that no prayer can pass through. You have made us filth and rubbish among the peoples" (*NRSV*).

All the normal feelings we experience are written about in the Bible. It helps to know, when we are in despair or confused, that these feelings are normal, that God understands and that provision has been made for solutions if we will look for them where they may be found. Consider Psalm 22, part of which Jesus cried out in anguish on the cross. The first line is, "My God, my God, why have you forsaken me?", and it goes on with descriptions of distress. Verse 19 is a prayer for help, and 21-24, a memory of a past rescue. The Psalm ends with others joining in praise for God's goodness. Throughout the whole Bible, these themes recur because they are based on life as it is lived.

Searchers need to be encouraged in their "vocation" of searching, but it is also necessary for them to connect with those who can lead them beyond the mere empirical facts to the spirit of the faith. John Wesley was a preacher and missionary before he felt his "heart strangely warmed" at Aldersgate. We never know when or how such a connection may occur, but that connection is the key to resolving a searcher's search and providing a joyful entry into partnership with God. Then the Bible can speak with a new authority, because it resonates with the faith of those who have diligently searched in the past and found their God to be, not only alive and well, but intimately acquainted with our innermost doubts and questions.

Questions to Consider

1. Does the Bible mean anything much to you?
2. Do new translations help you to understand? What do they lack?
3. Would a searcher's questions about the Bible embarrass or frighten you?
4. Is searching a satisfying or frustrating activity for you?

Resources for the Faith Journey

God is here—let's celebrate!
With song and with dance,
with stringed instruments and brass,
with cymbals and drums,
let us express ecstatic joy in God's presence.
Let us celebrate with the old songs of praise.
Let us also create new songs
that portray the eternal love of our God.

Leslie F. Brandt, Psalm 33:1-5,
Psalms Now, 53

I have opened this section with the above selection because it expresses some of the flavour of the partnership style. Celebration is a common experience, made even better by sharing the wonder of life with God with others. Partners are enabled to celebrate God's eternal love by both old and new songs. The Psalms, especially in new translations, reverberate in a partner's heart as she or he goes about daily tasks. As Brandt paraphrases later verses of Psalm 33, we see familiar expressions of biblical faith: "He did create this world. He continues to permeate it with His love.... God's love is sure and everlasting. Hearts open to His love are filled with joy. They truly find cause for celebration."[6]

Like many others who are now seniors, my biblical memory is of the *King James Version*. In addition to memory work in Sunday school, I began my ministry in 1953 when the *KJV* was used almost exclusively. The wonderful familiar passages in that elegant old English are still my path to meditation and to finding things in a concordance. More times than I could possibly recount, the familiar words have come to me in times of need, bringing reassurance, guidance, peace.

However, the Bible also brings us admonition and judgement.

Partners are not people who "have it all straight" and "never make mistakes." They need to sometimes search and change their ways and go through dark times of despair. What is different about them, as compared to searchers or community faithstyle persons, is that they know that they are loved and are able to make changes in how they express their faith without fear of getting lost. They connect with God at the core of their being.

The Bible introduces us to God's family and tells us what values the family lives by and what it has experienced in the past. Christianity was never meant to be a solitary faith. As a person moves ever deeper into the spiritual life, it seems other people become more real and the world surrounding us becomes a more urgent reality. As partners in faith, we have locked into the source of the power that enabled Jesus to come and to do what he did for all of us.

The Bible provides us with some wonderful examples of how God interacts with us. One of my favourites is the story of Elijah. After the great confrontations with Jezebel and the priests of Baal on Mount Carmel, Elijah's life is threatened and he flees to the desert (I Kings 19). He complains loudly to God that he has been the only faithful one, and now "they seek my life, to take it away." He is told to go and stand on the mountain of the Lord. Then "a great and strong wind rent the mountains and brake in pieces the rocks before the Lord; but the Lord was not in the wind. And after the wind an earthquake; but the Lord was not in the earthquake: And after the earthquake a fire; but the Lord was not in the fire: and after the fire a still small voice" (KJV). Theodore Lutz says that there is no adequate translation for the Hebrew words that the KJV translates as "still small voice." The closest we can come is something like "the sounds of silence." The NRSV translates it as "the sounds of sheer silence."

Elijah recognizes that God is in the silence, and he covers his face and goes to the mouth of the cave to confront God. He "hears": "What are you doing here, Elijah?" He answers: "I have been very zealous for the Lord, the God of hosts; for the Israelites have forsaken your covenant, thrown down your altars, and killed your prophets with the sword. I alone am left, and they are seeking my life, to take it away" (v.14, NRSV). How often do we feel alone and unable to do anything about a problem? We come complaining to God about it. We want comfort, reassurance, and sympathy, not more work to do! We may try to run away from the situation. At the end of verse 14, our instincts might tell us that Elijah deserves praise for his faithfulness. We might see him as a victim of evil and want to rescue him.

However, what does God do? Verse 15 begins: "Then the Lord said to him, 'Go, return on your way to the wilderness of Damascus; when you arrive, you shall anoint Hazael as king over Aram.'" The voice continues to give instructions in verse 16. Verse 17 mentions the help of Jehu and Elisha. Verse 18 states: "Yet I will leave seven thousand in Israel, all the knees that have not bowed to Baal, and every mouth that has not kissed him." So Elijah finds out that he is not alone, but that he has, in fact, a lot of work to do. He must be going to live!

Partners often report similar experiences of unexpected reactions, unexpected promises. Usually we "hear" best in the course of reflection, when we are still. Recall Psalm 46:10: "Be still, and know that I am God!" (both KJV and NRSV). In today's world, many people feel there is simply no time for this, yet such time is highly productive. It is not only good for our souls, but for our bodies. In the stillness, with the intuitive awareness of the reality of God (perhaps sharpened by a biblical passage), we experience a communication that is beyond description. There is a presence. I have sometimes felt enfolded in warmth and light. Usually I feel cleansed, renewed, strengthened. Often I feel directed or guided in particular ways. Sometimes I have arguments with God. I recently raised objections when I was prompted to go and do something. I "heard": "You've been praying for this thing for quite awhile now. If you really want it, go NOW!" I got up and went. I had been promised a significant meeting if I did so and it happened. Where the story goes from there remains to be seen. I frequently have to pray for patience!

I realize that to some people such experiences seem weird and questionable on a number of levels. I have no difficulty with the thought that they are related to the deep unconscious in each of us. However, I also have no difficulty with the thought that they are related to the "image of God" in us all. Discovering this reality and learning to live with it is infinitely easier if we immerse ourselves in the stories of God's relationships with people throughout the centuries. The Bible tells us what we can reasonably expect and how we might bring that about.

Jesus, for example, is emphatic about our need to decide in which direction we want to go. For example, in Luke 16:13, he says, "You cannot be the slave both of God and of money" (JB). He grieves for the rich man whose wealth makes him walk away from Jesus' invitation to follow him (Luke 18:18-25). In our consumeristic and competitive society, which flirts so outrageously with non-religious, if not non-Christian, values, we are in danger of losing our souls. If a man's worth is measured by his ability to earn "good money," and a woman's worth, by her slim attractiveness, where is there room for a connection with our Maker? Clearly, we have to go against the tide of popular opinion and make room. We must decide what really matters to us. A spiritual life requires more than a few minutes here and there while we are dashing around doing a multitude of things unrelated to our reason for living.

Jesus makes clear that once we have decided to be with him, we must be prepared to go with him into life as *he* knows it. We must allow our values to be changed. Among the most stunning of Jesus' statements are the ones concerning children:

Truly I tell you, unless you change and become like children, you will never enter the kingdom of heaven.

Whoever becomes humble like this child is the greatest in the kingdom of heaven. Whoever welcomes one such child in my name welcomes me. If any of you put a stumbling block before one of these little ones who believe in me, it would be better for you if a great millstone were fastened around your neck and you were drowned in the depth of the sea (Matt. 18:3-6, NRSV).

One of the important qualities of children is their eagerness, in healthy circumstances at least, to explore and experience new things. Children have an instinctive openness to spiritual reality, which can be very moving and beautiful. We can learn much from them about how to live in God's world with a sense of trust and expectancy. We are not, however, as Paul reminds us, to remain as children in our *thinking* (I Cor. 14:20). Paul talks a lot about growing up in the faith, for example, in Ephesians 4:11-14:

The gifts he gave were that some would be apostles, some prophets, some evangelists, some pastors and teachers, to equip the saints for the work of ministry, for building up the body of Christ, until all of us come to the unity of the faith and the knowledge of the Son of God, to maturity, to the measure of the full stature of Christ. We must no longer be children, tossed to and fro and blown about by every wind of doctrine, by people's trickery, by their craftiness in deceitful scheming (NRSV).

That last sentence reminds me of Jesus saying: "Be wise as serpents and innocent as doves" to the disciples as he sent them out on their mission (Matt. 10:16).

As we read and reflect on the ways God has worked with people through the ages, we realize that the Bible hardly suggests that we be other-worldly to the extent that we turn away from people, especially if they are in difficult circumstances. We are called to care for others, to do what we can for them with God's help. Partners in particular realize that a vital trust in God-beyond-themselves is necessary to discern what is not clear to us at any particular moment. Partners give themselves over to what God is trying to do through them. They may argue with God, and sometimes fall flat on their faces, but their goal is clear. At the end of *Faith Development and Pastoral Care*, James Fowler wrote:

> ... with Jesus' pointing to the in-breaking future of God's kingdom and to God's intended fulfillment of creation as the power of the future, we find ourselves grounded in time in a fundamentally new way. We begin to see that newness, possibility, and freedom come to us in each moment from God's future, as the gift of divine grace. We begin to see God as active in ongoing creation, governance, and lib-eration and redemption, luring and conserving creation toward God's future. And in renewed and sustained hope we turn toward our neighbor and stranger, and the encom-passing systems of our common lives, with refreshed vision and purpose and with re-grounded faith and vocation.[7]

Questions to Consider

1. Does the Bible seem dull to you? Perhaps only a history book?
2. In what ways can the Bible "come alive"?
3. Do you make use of Bible passages in times of trouble? Of joy?
4. Do you believe that the Bible can be a guide for your life?

Chapter Eight

Beliefs about the Holy Spirit

Threat, Comfort, or Joy?

> *"Spirit of God, descend upon my heart;*
> *wean it from earth, thro' all its pulses move;*
> *stoop to my weakness, strength to me impart,*
> *and make me love you as I ought to love.*
>
> George Croly,
> *Songs for a Gospel People*, #85[1]

In the week before Christmas, cars converged on the little church in the countryside. People of all ages emerged, with many teens clutching ukuleles. A spirit of expectation was in the air—among the children, because this was Jesus' birthday party, and among the adults, because they could finally hear the famous ukulele band in which many of their teens played. But this air of expectation in itself did not explain what happened that night. It was a truly joyful time. The spirited Christmas music, the baby on its mother's lap, the sense of togetherness, helped to make it thrilling beyond words. The teens in Canadian Girls in Training (C.G.I.T.) and their leaders discussed it later. "There was something there," said a leader. "I don't know what it was but there was *something*." All agreed. For several, it was their first experience of the lively presence of the Holy Spirit. In our United Church tradition, we seldom name the Holy Spirit as part of our services. Its immediacy and the wonder-filled experience it gave to the whole congregation were evidence of a real gift wrapped in a mystery.

Those who try to explain the Holy Spirit often become like the C.G.I.T. leader—aware of the reality, but unable to communicate it in words that can do justice to the experience. This may be partly why, although we pray for the presence of the Holy Spirit in most worship services in our mainline churches, we seldom talk about the presence of the spirit actually in and among us. Part of the reason may also be a basic distrust of emotion. We succumb to peer pressure to make sure everything is done "decently and in order." A common phrase for anything that is not is that someone got carried away. Getting carried away might mean a trip into a strange land for them, where it is not clear what may happen, where one does not know what to do, and, most importantly, where one may lose control.

It is this possible loss of even momentary control over one's life that truly terrifies the majority of people in our congregations and parishes. Community faithstyle persons share many of the same reservations, and feel far more secure within their closed group. Anyone who claimed that the Holy Spirit directed them to give all of their last Wheat Board payment to the poor, for example, would shake the very foundation of the logical, careful, and responsible approach typical of the community faithstyle, especially in rural congregations. "We can't do that," some would protest. Most of them would probably be uncomfortable knowing that Jesus did indeed suggest such things to his followers. The "so far and no farther" standard of the community stops anyone from "getting carried away" by being unnecessarily generous.

Getting "carried away" is a revealing phrase. It can mean

dancing recklessly at a local dance, beginning a disastrous pregnancy, speaking too long and/or bluntly at a public meeting, or appearing out of control in a church service. Anything that reveals a lack of normal self-control qualifies as excessive. Community faithstyle people have a deep devotion to self-control. It is probably one of their primary values. Therefore, in some circumstances, the Holy Spirit may be seen as a threat as much as a blessing. It's wonderful at a Christmas celebration where all are sharing a deeply moving experience of God coming to us in the baby Jesus and bringing joy, but it is terrible if it prompts someone to publicly take issue with the group.

A church board, for example, had a lively discussion on requesting government lottery funds for a project. The arguments for it made good business sense and many people from the community purchased tickets from that lottery. Then one female member spoke up. She strongly objected to the evil effects of lotteries and cited the biblical passage on how we are not to cause any weaker brother or sister to stumble (Rom. 14:21). She stressed how alien the idea of requesting lottery funds was when compared to the hard work of their ancestors in maintaining the church. She challenged them to think of their faith as a resource for making church decisions instead of being guided by what was acceptable in other parts of society. A long pause followed, while each person thought through their own belief and practice with regard to this issue. Finally, the chairperson said, "I guess we forget who we are sometimes," and the person who had spoken up said, "and the Holy Spirit tries to keep us on track."

Confrontational persons are particularly objectionable to some parishioners. In the community faithstyle, one is free to do many things without guilt, because "no one is going to call you on it" in the community at large. Anyone wanting to apply Christian standards in inconvenient ways is a nuisance at best, and a problem to be got rid of at worst. After all, Jesus was killed in part because he insisted that all of life is involved in a relationship with God. In many faith-communities, those who

111

won't "play the game right" are simply excluded from activities and frequently go somewhere else for worship and service. The Holy Spirit as a Comforter and Guide is much desired in times of distress or celebration, but not very welcome at other times!

In the beloved hymn that opens this section, the Spirit is asked to "wean" the heart from earth, to grant strength and "make me love you as I ought to love." These are typical community faithstyle sentiments. They hardly celebrate freedom of choice and co-operation, nor do they invite participation in the things of the world as parts of a living faith. They do, however, express dependence on God's working in us to help us to do our appointed tasks.

We often confuse the work of the Holy Spirit with "conscience." Conscience is a product of our upbringing and reflects our society's values. Claude Brown, raised in the slums of New York, gives us a clear picture of this:

> When I was a little boy, Mama and Dad would beat me and tell me "you better be good", but I didn't know what good was. To me, it meant that they wanted me to sit down and fold my hands or something crazy like that. Stay in front of the house, don't go anyplace, don't get into trouble. I didn't know what it meant and I don't think they knew what it meant, because they couldn't ever tell me what they really wanted.
>
> The way I saw it, everything I was doing was good. If I stole something and didn't get caught, I was good. If I got into a fight with somebody I tried to be good and beat him. If I broke into a place, I tried to be quiet and steal as much as I could. I was always trying to be good.[2]

It is important that Christians learn how to separate the work of the Holy Spirit from the work of conscience. These two may be in agreement on some things, but disagree strongly on others. The Methodists had a whole system for "discerning the Spirit," because they recognized that any person can be confused or misled by something that seems to be of the Holy Spirit, but is not. Ideas were tested by reflection on the Bible and by prayer, but also by reason and tradition. The possibility of "getting carried away" by other spirits was clearly acknowledged. We need a good grounding and to be aware of the possibilities involved in order to be sure that we are in touch with the living God.

Some common experiences of the Holy Spirit among community faithstyle people may not be recognized as such. "I just felt I had to" or "I couldn't shake the idea" or "It dawned on me that…" are all expressions that often imply spiritual experiences or intuitions. The essential element is that it is "given." It does not arise from one's own being as far as one can tell. The stories that follow such admissions are usually stories of a need met or an important time shared.

Take Mary Jones, for example, who was on her way home from work one day and suddenly felt a strong pull to visit her friend Joan. She told herself she would call her after dinner. But when she arrived at the crossroad between her home and Joan's, she found herself turning towards Joan's. She found Joan in a really deep depression, planning suicide. She had not been aware of the despair at the core of Joan's life. Or take Eric Timber, who told of being "at the end of his rope" with family and personal troubles, kneeling by a kitchen chair, pouring it all out to God. "It just came over me," he reported, "the most wonderful peace I have ever known. I have never doubted since then that God knows and cares and will help when I need it."

There are countless numbers of such stories in our congregations and parishes, but they are not always shared. The reason may be partly an unwillingness to "stand out" from the group in any way and partly a fear that others would not understand and would somehow damage the meaning of it for us. It may also simply be that we want to hold this precious treasure as a kind of touchstone to help us through rough times. Whatever the reason, there is no doubt that some of the most important spiritual resources of our congregations are never shared.

In terms of Paul's teaching concerning gifts being given to the Church so that all needs can be met (Rom. 12:6-8; I Cor. 12:4-31), it is clear that this lack of sharing is an important roadblock to fullness of life for congregations. If we cannot trust each other enough to share meaningful experiences, we block ourselves from any possible growth and enjoyment. Imagine a spring with pebbles accumulating across its outflow path. As the little dam grows higher and stronger, the flow of water bringing refreshment and life to those further down its path is cut off. The life that needs the fresh water becomes polluted and will finally die if no help comes. This is the situation in many community faithstyle churches. The Spirit is working among the people, but they are not willing or able to share what is happening. They are busy holding on to old forms—even while new life arises within. It is choked off instead of expressed.

Events like the Christmas party, where everyone can bask in the blessing of the Spirit's presence—at no cost to themselves—are much more acceptable to community faithstyle persons than the risk of sharing their experiences. If the Holy Spirit confined its work to such joyous events, there would be ready acceptance of it. However, we know the Spirit is also the provoker of new thoughts, the guide into new paths, and the one who makes it possible for us to live in harmony with God in our daily lives. For many people, that is too much to take. It interferes with our own plans and the lives we have carved out of what is "expected" of us. The Holy Spirit's invitation to new life is only welcome, to many, if the new life is basically like the old. We have forgotten Jesus' comment about patching old wine bottles: Dry old leather won't accept a pliant new patch (Mark 2:22).

It is tragic when so many who struggle daily with burdens that nearly overwhelm them have unused resources right at hand. If only they would stop their frantic activities and worrying for at least a few moments each day and learn the benefits of stillness in God's presence, they could learn to tap into that energy God has provided for us. If people do take time for Quiet Time, they often fill it with reading or a prayer that they memorized long ago. There is nothing wrong with this, but it is clearly not enough. Imagine visiting a friend and not discussing what is going on with the both of you. You wouldn't have a real visit at all. Only as we allow ourselves to be still in God's presence can we hear "the still, small voice" of the Spirit. Only when we let ourselves physically relax does the pressure ease and release new thoughts and feelings.

A pressure cooker sending up steam does not allow anything to enter it. Many of our lives are like that. The wonderful fresh blessing from the springs of living water can only come to us when we let them flow over us, and calm us inside, so we can open our lives to the reality of God reaching to us. That is the wonderful and ever-renewable surprise: as we open ourselves to God we discover that God is ready and willing to meet us where we truly are. The Holy Spirit leads us, when we allow it, right to the heart of God. In the words of John Donne:

> God never says, you should have come yesterday;
> God never says, you must come again to-morrow,
> but today if you will hear God's voice,
> today God will hear you....[3]

Questions to Consider

1. Have you had experiences one might call spiritual? If so, did you share them? Why or why not?
2. Is the name "Holy Spirit" helpful? Is it easier for us to use "God" or "Jesus" instead?
3. Are you afraid of being asked to change?
4. Have you found it to be true that God is reaching out to us? Does it matter what word we use for this—which person of the Trinity?

Sorting out the Human and Divine

From my earliest childhood
the need to possess some "absolute"
was the pivot of all my inner life.

. . . .

Sometimes ... I would take delight
in the thought of God/Spirit
(at the time, the Flesh of Christ
seemed to me too fragile, too corruptible).
...I had at that time an irresistible need
(both life-giving and consoling) to come to rest forever
in something tangible and definite.
And I searched everywhere for this beatifying Object.
The story of my inner life is summed up in this search,
ever dwelling on realities
more and more universal and perfect.
Fundamentally this deep natural tendency has
    remained
absolutely unchanged ever since I began to know
    myself.

Teilhard de Chardin[4]

Teilhard de Chardin is famous throughout the world for his integrated thinking on God and science in the universe. He came to believe that "all things are now but one." The quotation above expresses something that searchers are well aware of—the urge to find something tangible and definite in which to rest forever, the tendency to feel that it is possible "to settle the matter once and for all." De Chardin would tell them that longing is a lost cause. Furthermore, he said, "Our concept of God must be extended as the dimensions of our world are extended."[5] Since our "worldly" knowledge seems to be increasing very rapidly it stands to reason that our concept of God needs to expand at the same time.

One of the major ways of coming to know God is through the nature and activities of the Holy Spirit. Because the life of the Spirit is not tangible, it is particularly hard for searchers to understand. They frequently believe that if they feel the lively presence of the Spirit, it is arising from them or from their circumstances. Young persons may be moved by modern music, which can be quite unappealing to older people. In turn, older persons may be moved by family events of celebration, or new birth. It may not be possible or easy for them to acknowledge the reality of something beyond themselves that is adding to their experience.

The Holy Spirit's "signature" is a sense of connection with a deeper, longer-lasting reality than a purely non-religious event offers. Other words come to mind that are sometimes used to describe such events: One of them is "awe," another, "a sense of the holy." Awe is defined as "reverential fear," a sense of meeting a powerful energy. The sense of the holy may be profoundly still, or some may think of it as a particular atmosphere. Both of these are related to the hushed voices often used when visiting cathedrals. While I was travelling in England, I discovered that the voices were more hushed in places where worship was still held. Where the cathedrals had become tourist attractions, with expert guides to explain it all, there was rarely such an atmosphere.

According to a recent theory, building materials are thought to absorb some of the reality of what has happened around them. Those who investigate ghosts are particularly interested in this. I have always sensed that a church in which God has been worshipped in spirit and in truth over the years must absorb something, because when inside it, one can sometimes feel surrounded by a presence that is clearly from another dimension.

Such experiences have been studied from many different

viewpoints. William James, chemist, physician, then psychologist and philosopher, studied and wrote about religion in general as a phenomenon of human nature. He gave the Gifford Lectures in Edinburgh in 1901-1902. The famous book in which his classic lectures are published is called *The Varieties of Religious Experience*. In the twentieth lecture, entitled Conclusions, he sums up the characteristics of the religious life. It includes the following beliefs:

1. That the visible world is part of a more spiritual universe from which it draws its chief significance;
2. That union or harmonious relation with that higher universe is our true end;
3. That prayer or inner communion with the spirit thereof—be that spirit 'god' or 'law'—is a process wherein work is really done, and spiritual energy flows in and produces effects, psychological or material, within the phenomenal world.

Religion also includes the following psychological characteristics:

4. A new zest which adds itself like a gift to life, and takes the form either of lyrical enchantment or of appeal to earnestness and heroism.
5. An assurance of safety and a temper of peace, and, in relation to others, a preponderance of loving affections.[6]

In the 1960s and 1970s, psychologist Abraham Maslow studied and wrote about religion in general as a phenomenon of human nature. Maslow specialized in "peak-experiences." He believes that "to the extent that all mystical or peak-experiences are the same in their essence and have always been the same, all religions are the same in their essence and always have been the same. They should, therefore, come to agree in principle on teaching that which is common to all of them...."[7]

Maslow has an interesting theory about the work of ministry: He says that each religion has been founded by what he calls a "peaker"—someone who is in touch with the universal underlying reality. The people who work with this revelation in churches, for example, are often "organization men" who are "non-peakers." Consequently, the original, intended message gets lost, and instead of remaining a primarily spiritual message, it becomes "concretized." For example, people make their words and ceremonies into sacred things and sacred activities. The concretizations "finally become hostile to the original mystical experiences." Furthermore, in Maslow's words, "most religions have wound up denying and being antagonistic to the very ground upon which they were originally based."[8]

It seems clear to me that Jesus was well aware of the universal God who becomes known in peak experiences: using his name is like having a card of introduction. In John 14, Jesus announces the coming of the Holy Spirit: "... the Advocate, the Holy Spirit whom the Father will send in my name, will teach you everything, and remind you of all that I have said to you" (John 14:26, NRSV). The Spirit is sometimes called The Spirit of Truth (v.17), the Comforter (v.26, KJV), the Advocate (v.26, NRSV). Jesus is clearly linking himself to the eternal Spirit, which has been in the world from the beginning with God (Isa. 40:13).

Community faithstyle persons often feel anger or frustration with those who even read about such things, let alone believe them! The possibility of meeting a universal God in an experience similar to the experience of conversion seems to them not only dangerous but evil. Yet searchers will find it helpful to know that God has created our ability to know Godself in a variety of ways. They may then begin to explore which one of the available faiths is most in line with their own growing convictions. They may not always arrive at the family's decision, and this may be a great sorrow.

The whole experience is made more difficult with the knowledge that some psychologists and psychoanalysts view religion as a bad influence. In fact, a recent poll showed that only about half have any appreciation of religion at all. Sigmund Freud, the founder of psychoanalysis, wrote a book about religious beliefs entitled *The Future of an Illusion*. The truth of the matter seems to be that his judgements had been formed on the basis of its effects on people who were ill. As Maslow points out, "inner voices, the 'revelations', may be mistaken ... and there is then no way of finding out whether the voices within are the voices of good or evil.... Spontaneity (the impulses from our best self) gets confused with impulsivity and acting out (the impulses from our sick self), and there is then no way to tell the difference."[9]

Christians need to be honest about such difficulties. They have inherited a long tradition of "testing the Spirit" in the history of Christian communities. John Wesley, for example, demanded tests of reason and tradition as well as of prayer and the Bible. In one community in which I served, I heard about the "testing" of a candidate for the ministry that had taken place across from the manse in a now non-existent building. Some of the very old people remembered with awe how the young man's call was examined. There was clearly a sense of the Spirit being at work that night. Searchers need to know about the care that is exercised to ensure that the faith is not contaminated by beliefs that are inconsistent with Jesus' teachings or Christian tradition. These concerns need to be taken more seriously by all Christians. We are seeing increasingly lax practices of faithfulness, and searchers have a very low tolerance for people who say one thing and do another in their faith life.

As Teilhard de Chardin told us at the beginning, searchers are looking for tangible signs of something that will give them satisfaction and security. If they have a peak-experience, they may very well want to know more about its meaning. They may then want to become acquainted with the Christian doctrine of the Holy Spirit. To communicate with God, through the Holy Spirit, is indeed a very special privilege, available to everyone!

Questions to Consider

1. What picture is in your mind's eye when you say, "Holy Spirit"?
2. Does it seem to make our Holy Spirit less important if we believe, like Maslow, that other people can have similar experiences with a universal reality?
3. Would you like to feel at one with the universe and all its people?
4. Would it be possible for you to keep talking to a searcher who was having these experiences?

The Spirit's Gifts Within

Truthful Spirit, dwell with me!
I myself would truthful be;
And, with wisdom kind and clear,
Let Thy life in mine appear;
And, with actions brotherly,
Speak my Lord's sincerity.

Thomas Toke Lynch,
The Hymnary, #152

When I checked "The Holy Spirit" section of *The Hymnary*, the hymn book I used for twenty years in the ministry, I was startled to realize that we had never sung the above hymn. "Breathe on me, Breath of God" and "Spirit of God, descend upon my heart" were great favourites. They are very personal and very much in keeping with the community faithstyle of worship. When *The Hymn Book* was published in 1971, I discovered "As comes the breath of spring" and then found it in *The Hymnary* as well. It begins: "As comes the breath of spring / With light, and mirth, and song, / So does God's Spirit bring / New days—brave, free and strong." What a good hymn for searchers, I think now, but also for partners. We have used it quite a bit in the last ten years. However, community faithstyle persons have not enjoyed it to the same extent. It has too much energy, too broad a vision, and too much threat of change!

As I consider now the path of my own faith journey, I realize that although I am involved in deep and meaningful new experiences of God's active presence, I still like many old hymns and practices. I listen to the CBC "Hymn Sing" programme of old favourites whenever I can, as it touches something deep within me. I also, however, love the modern songs and hymns that are more reflective of the world in which we now live.

I have never been more conscious of the ways in which we

need to grow in faith. As I meditate, I sometimes remember how the "contemplative life" used to mean a life divorced from the world. I am constantly brought up short by the realization that, in communion with God, one is connected with other realities of life in the universe. "When you get to God, you get sent out to help with God's work in the world," someone has said. One's own needs are met in many Grace-filled ways, but there is an openness to God's will that makes one concerned with meeting others' needs as well.

In *God and Human Suffering*, Douglas John Hall states that "Jesus' invitation to 'Come, follow me' ... is simply an invitation to *life*.... It is not an invitation to heaven but to earth, not to church but to life in the world. It is an invitation and permission to take up in all consciousness, and in gratitude, the *creaturely* life that is our destiny. To become who we are."[10] To a partner, the Holy Spirit is the truth-bearing guide in this whole endeavour. Dag Hammarskjold described this in his book *Markings*: "The more faithfully you listen to the voice within you, the better you will hear what is sounding outside."[11]

Partners normally try to arrange definite periods of time to be open to the Spirit. They may go on organized retreats as well as privately and daily meditating and praying. They may meet with a spiritual director or with a small group involved in deepening their spiritual life. They may read or go for walks or explore a forest or garden. Anything, as Madeleine d'Engle's books show, can become a base for reflection or contemplation. Openness to the Spirit, and allowing oneself to interact with the Spirit, makes the partnership relationship possible.

If one wishes to track the growth of such a life, Dietrich Bonhoeffer's books can help. Bonhoeffer was a prisoner of war during World War II. The conditions in the prison were dreadful, but he was allowed to receive books and write letters, articles, and books. Bonhoeffer had led a privileged life, and he was gifted and ambitious. As a result of his internment, he gradually became a man who identified with others in a way he could never have done before. He developed an idea of what the Christian faith might become. This he called "religionless Christianity." He saw, all too clearly, how the ways in which people tried to be obedient to religious systems prevented their real connection with God. He would have agreed with Hall's statement that "we have only to become honest, to allow ourselves to become real. Discipleship means sacrificing all the little defenses and stratagems by which we shield ourselves from life, and accepting freely and gladly the gift of life *as it is given to us.*"[12]

When we reflect on this, we realize that the efforts of community faithstyle persons to make good impressions, as well as the efforts of searchers to understand everything, can be self-defeating if they prevent the development of a relationship of trust in God that will allow them to open to their true inner selves. The core of the matter is the recognition of change within—of new life developing, of hope replacing despair, of direction replacing meaninglessness. While community faithstyle persons generally emphasize repentance and forgiveness of sin, partners are more likely to celebrate the discovery of who they really are and can become. As the hymn "As Comes the Breath of Spring" puts it: "... his [God's Spirit's] joy shines forth and then / Life blossoms to its goal."

This is a major difference in the quality of life among partners as compared to the other faithstyles. Partners seem to trust the naturalness of their development—an unfolding—rather than a forced discipline. Instead of consciously working on remembering all the rules, one works on trusting the Spirit to explore and discern what is possible *now*. It reminds me of Jesus' saying, "My yoke is easy, my burden is light." A partner is more aware of the challenges in the world, but also more empowered to deal with them in terms of their own strength and gifts.

Partners have a capacity to care for others in a deep way because they have become acquainted with their own depths.

They have the patience to listen without judging or trying to provide an immediate solution; they have the love to hold someone through their tears. Of course, not everyone is at the same stage of growth, but these are the directions in which partners move. When a person has come into meaningful relationship with the Holy Spirit, they have more than their own power and wisdom to draw from.

Often a marked shift towards hope and humility is evident when a person moves into partnership. A searcher may have been desperately seeking any meaning in life, while a community faithstyle person may have been struggling to "keep up appearances." The work of the Spirit affirms each person's real value and possibilities. They are given a new base for their life. Since this base is a gift of the Spirit, they are more accepting of both their limits and their potential, at one and the same time. Hence, they are not only more realistic but also more grateful! As Dag Hammarskjold said:

> For all that has been,
> Thanks!
> For all that will be,
> Yes![13]

Questions to Consider

1. Does the work of the Holy Spirit seem confusing in terms of its union with or separation from God and Jesus?
2. Have you ever thought of this energy as Grace? Does it matter what we call the Holy Spirit?
3. Does the life of the partner seem like a desirable one? Why?
4. Are there some ways in which you know you could move towards this style if you felt so inclined?

Chapter Nine

Understandings of Sin and Forgiveness

The Struggle to be "Good"

Just as I am, without one plea
But that thy blood was shed for me,
And that thou bidd'st me come to Thee,
O Lamb of God, I come.

Just as I am, Thou wilt receive,
Wilt welcome, pardon, cleanse, relieve;
Because Thy promise I believe,
O Lamb of God, I come.

Charlotte Elliott,
The Hymnary, #270

An attractive young woman is weeping. "I know I shouldn't," she blurts out, "but I can't stand it when my in-laws assume my husband will do whatever *they* want. I get angry." An older man is talking with a neighbour. "I got rid of that car the other day— the one that couldn't pass the safety check. Sold it to a young lad from Lake Road. Got five hundred dollars for it. He thought it looked great."

Sin, so obvious to us sometimes and yet so well concealed at others, is a preoccupation for some community faithstyle persons. Like the young woman quoted above, many believe that strong emotions, such as anger, are sinful. They block them. The result can be dis-ease, tension, and terror. They fear what would happen if they ever lost control. They know that Jesus pointed out that bad actions have their origins in thought or feeling. They sometimes feel "dirty clear through" because of real or imagined bad thoughts. Traditional Roman Catholics have a word for this: "scrupulosity." The sufferer does all the right and prescribed things carefully, but feels they are never enough. Nothing is ever enough. Guilt remains like sludge at the bottom of a pond. They cannot forgive themselves or let themselves accept forgiveness.

The older man quoted above seems to be at the opposite extreme. He not only excuses his immoral action, he brags about it. He does not think about the implication of his actions on another person's life. His attitude is that people should look out for themselves. Taking responsibility for yourself means learning how not "to be taken." Some may say, "It's a dog-eat-dog-world." Normally such persons are more careful in their treatment of others in their own community than they are with strangers, but not always. They may be "good" members of their community and church. They simply have God locked up in that same cage we described earlier. God is not to interfere with everyday life, but is relegated to church and special occasions.

In the Bible, sin has a number of meanings. *Harper's Bible Dictionary* defines sin as "that which is in opposition to God's benevolent purposes for his creation." The article points out that "the concept of sin is first and foremost a religious concept, because all sin is ultimately against God, God's laws, God's creation, God's covenant, and God's purposes. It is the basic corrupting agent in the entire universe."[1] This aspect of sin is frequently overlooked in the lives of community faithstyle persons, because their particular practices, often shared over many years, are judged by practical consequences in their local community. If someone called the man who sold the unfit car a sinner, for example, he would be likely to ask, "What has God got to do with it?" He might think that the young man and his family could rightly have a grievance against him, but surely he had not hurt God! After all, he had not broken one of the Ten Commandments.

The Hebrew word meaning "a deliberate act of defiance" is most commonly used in the Old Testament for "sin." Community faithstyle persons tend to adopt this sort of definition: it has to be something bad that you did, with full knowledge that it was bad, to be called a sin. Then when you come to God, you simply admit it and are forgiven. The words of the hymn "Just As I Am" are dearly loved because they clearly reflect this way of dealing with sin. For many, it is simply a moral transaction with God.

There are, however, other sins: failure to attend church or observe the correct rituals (such as having your baby baptized); not doing what you know God wants done or doing the wrong thing (missing the mark of God's will); hating, envying, being selfish or otherwise hurtful to other people; being a hypocrite. All of these may be judged as more of a sin against the community than against God, but they all carry considerable weight. The "biggy," however, is the "unforgivable sin" (Matt. 12:32). Jesus is clearly referring to a sin against the Holy Spirit—a denial of its reality and its power. The idea is frequently understood however, to mean that it is *possible* to do something so bad that you can never be forgiven. Those who already have low self-esteem may dwell on this and even make themselves sick over it. The actual transgression can be minor, but the person cannot be healed without discovering what lies behind their reaction.

Most of us recognize other groups of sins related to Jesus' call to live a life of discipleship: the parable of the sheep and the goats (Matt. 25:31-46), for example, emphatically states that we are punished if we do not care for the needy around us; the parable of the talents (Matt. 25:14-30) tells us that we must use the abilities and the resources that we have; the statements about taking up a cross and following Jesus (Mark 8:34-38) include the idea of giving up one's life in faithfulness to the gospel. These are the sorts of things with which community faithstyle persons may really struggle. What do faithful persons do, for example, when all of their neighbours are, like them, without an extra dollar or an extra hour to help the needy? What does a person do when he or she can play the organ for church and there is no one else who can do it, but this same person is also overextended beyond coping with the demands of their own family life? What kind of sacrifice is Jesus talking about when he talks of giving up one's life to someone who is strained to the limit by just trying to get the chores done? We need to talk about these things. They are everyday realities for most people and they need the perspective of others' understandings of Jesus' real message. There is an enormous amount of free-floating guilt around in community faithstyle circles.

Paul provides us with lists of sins, but we need to keep the regions in which Paul was working in mind. Where he worked, Christians were faced with many temptations. The orgies of some Greek mystery religions would rival anything that our most free-wheeling movies might contain today. Paul was concerned about the religious effects of becoming immersed in such things. He knew that Christians could be led astray. The lists contain a variety of prohibitions. Galatians 5:19 (NRSV) is typical:

> Now the works of the flesh are obvious: fornication [sex outside of marriage], impurity, licentiousness [lustfulness], idolatry, sorcery, enmities, strife, jealousy, anger, quarrels, dissensions, factions, envy, drunkenness, carousing, and

things like these. I am warning you, as I warned you before: those who do such things will not inherit the kingdom of God.

Now that "hits home"! People can live without adultery, for example, but in our society at least one family member is likely to have sex without commitment at some point in his or her life. Are we capable of avoiding all the types of disagreements mentioned? Is not anger sometimes good and necessary? Do we not have to disagree with people who are doing wrong and even work against them? Community faithstyle persons need, desperately at times, to talk about such things with those who understand what Paul was doing and, at the same time, appreciate the moral dilemmas of our children and grandchildren. Will they really be banished from the kingdom of God? What does that mean? Will they make it to heaven? If not, what will become of them? Is there a fiery hell to which the damned go? What kind of God would send people there for some of the aforementioned actions? Any pastor in this day and age knows how wrenching these questions can be for parishioners.

The Bible tells us that sin is universal. Much of the biblical material deals with it in terms of how God views it. The Adam and Eve story with its "Original Sin" is particularly important to community faithstyle persons, but they do not think it is fair for other people to suffer because of the sin of those first two! They do recognize, however, that we are not born with instincts that make it easy to "be good." The drive to survive can make even young children very competitive and demanding of others. Sexuality is a major issue of concern, especially in homes where this is not discussed or treated in a healthy way. The covering of the genitals in the Adam and Eve story suggests to many that sex is the original sin. This is extremely confusing, to say the least. Animals, birds, fish, and insects in the natural world around us practice sex as a completely good and natural thing.

Whatever community faithstyle individuals think about sexuality, they are not likely to ignore it. Life as such, family and community life in particular, is central to their experience. They may need to be reminded that in the beginning God created all things and declared them good. This includes biological realities, such as the need for food and sex. There needs to be a great deal more acceptance and appreciation of our human bodies as the gifts that they are. The Bible tells us that sex is a meaningful way of relating to one another as well as for "begetting" the human race, as Genesis informs us. The long tradition of silence, embarrassment, and guilt about our physical bodies has undoubtedly resulted in more, rather than less, inappropriate sexual activity. Sin enters the picture when sex is used to exploit or harm another person or oneself.

Paul gives us another list in Galatians (5:22,23,25, NRSV)— only this time he describes the effects that faithfulness to Christ brings: "By contrast, the fruit of the Spirit is love, joy, peace, patience, kindness, generosity, faithfulness, gentleness, and self-control. There is no law against such things…. If we live by the Spirit, let us also be guided by the Spirit." How do we get from sin to enjoyment of these effects? For community faithstyle persons, the most familiar way may be through the altar call type of event. This experience has three definite stages: the arousal of guilt, the willingness to admit publicly that something is wrong and a change is desired, and the acceptance of the ministrations of a leader or priest. In the mainline churches, such services are no longer generally used. These churches choose a General Confession in worship and offer private counselling if requested. United Church of Canada ministers are not generally trained to do formal confession or absolution rites, which are familiar to Roman Catholics and many Anglicans. The result is that there is an assumption that all people in a congregation are at the same level of peace with their God. In The United Church of Canada Communion Service, the minister may say:

Here is good news for you.
Christ Jesus came into the world to save sinners.
If we confess our sins, he is just, and may be trusted to
forgive our sins and cleanse us from every kind of wrong.
So it is that I can assure you that your sins are forgiven.[2]

The 1984 *A Sunday Liturgy for Optional Use* has the following evasion of "sin/forgiveness" in its assurance of pardon:

Anyone in Christ becomes a new person altogether.
The past is finished and gone;
everything has become fresh and new.
Friends, believe the good news of the gospel.

This is unsatisfactory for some community faithstyle persons. In the preceding prayer from *A Sunday Liturgy*, the congregation has confessed to being "in bondage to sin and [we] cannot free ourselves," followed by specific types of sin, such as, "We have not loved you with our whole heart; we have not loved our neighbour as ourselves." This prayer of confession ends with: "Forgive us, renew us, and lead us so that we may delight in your will and walk in your ways, to the glory of your holy name."[3] I mention these things because they represent some of the changes in thought patterns of modern mainline churches. What is missing in *A Sunday Liturgy* is the *authority* of the minister or priest. Despite many efforts of churches to downplay that authority, the community faithstyle person still generally likes to know that someone with authority has offered forgiving words.

I have observed other difficulties in the treatment of sin in modern mainline churches. Remember the altar call pattern—the personal decision to seek release from sin and its consequences, the personal action involved in going forward, the acceptance of the ministry offered? I believe that that type of service should be available in some form for those who would like to experience it. Part of my reason for recommending this is because when I began to lead occasional communion services with intinction (coming forward to break off a piece of bread and dip it in the grape juice), many people admitted they liked it because they had to make a decision. The young people especially said that it was just too easy to sit and be served. They said it felt like they made a declaration of faith when they got up and came forward. We *need* more action-oriented rites. We cannot always assume that we know what is going on in every parishioner's spiritual life.

How do we get from Paul's list of sins to his list of "fruits of the Spirit"? There are many ways. Some of them are deeply personal and individuals prefer to keep them private. However, others are looking for opportunities to acknowledge, perhaps in private conversation with their minister or priest, or perhaps before the congregation, that something really has changed for them. And when they do that we need to have appropriate words to celebrate the experience. We also need to follow up such an event and encourage the growth of the person involved.

Generally speaking, we do not experience a once-and-for-all forgiveness. At unpredictable times, a Christian feels "convicted" of different sorts of sin. This is a natural part of growth in the life of the Spirit. As Keith Miller, a lay evangelist and group leader, has pointed out, "all a man does when he commits his 'whole life' is to commit that of which he is conscious."[4] As we grow closer to God through Christ and the Spirit, we become more and more conscious of both the good and the bad in ourselves. We rejoice at the possibilities God gives us. Forgiveness opens a lot of doors and lets a lot of pleasure back in.

Many community faithstyle persons, as I have indicated elsewhere, have a strong appreciation for the role of the crucified Jesus in all of this. They have a depth of appreciation for the gift of life that Jesus brings that is beyond description. Anyone working with their concerns about sin and salvation needs to understand that both sin and forgiveness are very concrete things to most community faithstyle persons. They are not interested so much in the theories as in the effects. The theology of the cross comes later.

Questions to Consider

1. In what way do you believe, or not, that Jesus died for you?
2. When you feel guilty, do you think about the God-connection?
3. Is it a sin to follow the normal practices of your community even if you think they are wrong in God's eyes? How do you know?
4. Would you like to have some other ways of expressing your faith than your church normally offers?

From Commandments to Love

> *Christian theology has always insisted that sin is not our created state. It is precisely for this reason that theology makes the distinction between creation and fall. The human creature is not created sinful. Yet one must admit that the potentiality for sin is certainly already present in the creaturely condition and, apparently, as a matter of divine intention.*
>
> Douglas John Hall,
> *God and Human Suffering,* 56

With characteristic curiosity, searchers seek out explanations for the strange paradox of Christian faith: God is good and has made a good world, yet bad things still happen to the people God supposedly loves. On the surface, it does not make much sense. No wonder the doctrine of original sin was accepted as an explanation for so long—"You gotta blame somebody!"—and Adam and Eve were convenient targets. They *do* take God off the hook by deliberately disobeying a rule God had made for them. Creation was perfect until that woman and man thought it would be exciting to have the same knowledge of good and evil that God possessed. They did not accept "their place."

In *God and Human Suffering,* Hall offers some new insights into the Adam and Eve story. He states that we need to look at what God created and what God's intention were in this story. Our lives are clearly not meant to be trouble-free. Hall says that human beings have four basic experiences that may lead to sin: loneliness (Adam without Eve), limitation (don't eat from that tree!), temptation (the serpent and the apple), and anxiety (being caught, and being expelled). He states that "not *all* of what we experience as suffering is totally absurd, a mistake, an oversight, or the consequence of sin." He then goes on to explore what life would be like without these things. We would lose the opposite experiences. First of all, we would not know "the joy of human fellowship" and love. We would not experience "wonder, surprise, or gratitude." Furthermore, we would be "programmed to be good." And finally, we would never "know comfort, relief, or joy."[5]

Hall's thoughts may give searchers some fresh food for reflection. Since they often begin searching from within the community faithstyle, searchers frequently feel confusion about the creation and the fall. They may very well have been taught that we are "evil clear through." In fact Reformed (Protestant) theology teaches that human beings are a mixture of good and evil. No one can be without sin. I remember a professor telling us once that we are like a muddy river: you can't separate out rocks of evil and allow the stream of life to flow clear and good.

Searchers, influenced by modern psychology, may object to that teaching. For many years now, some authorities have argued that we are born not only innocent but good. Only our environment makes us bad. Searchers may consider this a proof that indeed we did not "fall" with Adam and Eve so that evil is built into human nature. They have observed the effects of belief in inherited human evil on people they know.

I have talked with people who were brought up in ultra-conservative homes where there was never any suggestion that there could be anything good about them at all. One individual reported that his parents wanted him and his siblings to be "depressed all the time." Intrigued, I asked him to explain, and he said, "Well, they just wanted us to sit there and do nothing, to be good." Many of us were reared with the belief that children should be seen and not heard. To be "good" seemed to mean that we would make no demands on adults. Many children had their parents try to "beat the evil out of them." After all, the Bible says, "Those who spare the rod hate their children, but those who love them are diligent to discipline them" (Prov. 13:24, NRSV). Searchers may be trying to find a way of dealing with the traumatic effects of such psychological and emotional abuse in their own lives. Thus, it may be very hard for them to consider the idea, let alone feel the reality, that God is a loving father.

Searchers are often seeking an ideal solution to their personal problems, societal problems, and those of the world at large. They are eager, therefore, to do away with anything that seems to get in the way of "happiness"—any religious practice or belief that has proven to be destructive to some. This has caused a swing away from discipline and doctrine. Searchers want freedom, equality, and room to move in the direction they choose. They simply dismiss the beliefs that trouble them—such as "the myth of Adam and Eve."

Actually, searchers would be well advised to study the nature of "myths." Myths would not exist if they did not speak to the elemental realities in our lives. They express truth in a different way. Myths are not history, nor psychology, nor wisdom literature; rather, as Northrop Frye says, "myths are the functional units of human society."[6] If we want evidence of that we might consider some of the myths that influence us: "Men are strong and women are weak"; "Children will grow up just fine if we don't frustrate them"; "Churches are essential to keep society moral"; "A person has reached perfection when he or she has no troubles in life."

Sin as an offense against God does not exist as a reality to the searcher, of course, while he or she is denying, or doubting, that there is a God. Sin becomes simply the bad things that people and societies inflict on one another. A person is accountable for these sins in this world only. An individual may be taken to court, lose their profession or their marriage, or may get away with gross exploitation, meanness, or selfishness. If successful, one may even be admired by others who yearn for positions of such power and freedom. The pragmatism of "whatever works" is frequently considered valuable in our society. Yet searchers often become involved in fighting the evils of hunger, pollution, war, and the like, and are by no means without conscience or concern.

If a searcher decides to look deeper, she or he may find it fascinating to discover how others define sin. Community faithstyle persons are likely to inform the searcher that God has made the world to run on certain principles which may be found in the Bible. With regard to sin, there are Ten Commandments that must not be broken. We are also commanded by Jesus to "love one another as I have loved you" (John 15:12). This makes life a lot more enjoyable. If a partnership style person is interviewed, the answers may be very different. The words of Jesus on love are likely to be considered more important to searchers than the Ten Commandments. However, the primary difference for partners is likely to be their awareness of sin in the ongoing interaction between God and the particular person. Pride, for example, may cause a person to want to take over the controls and do whatever he or she feels like doing, regardless of the consequences.

In the seventh century, Gregory the Great formulated a list of sins that were later called the Seven Deadly Sins. Searchers might find these to be useful guides to what is thought to be a good, healthy relationship with God. Theologian Karl H. Peschke notes that "they are called 'capital' not because they are always necessarily grave, but because they easily become vices and sources of many other sins." The list is:

Pride—desire for "honour, distinction and independence. It is opposed to the virtue of humility."

Avarice—"inordinate pursuit of material goods ... contrary to the virtues of liberality and equity."

Envy—"discontent over the good of one's neighbour, which is considered as a detriment to one's own person. It offends against brotherliness and magnanimity."

Lust—"the inordinate craving for sexual gratification ... is against the virtue of chastity."

Gluttony—"excess in the enjoyment of food and drink; the opposite virtues are temperance and sobriety."

Anger—"the intemperate outburst of dislike with the inordinate desire for another's punishment. It is contrary to patience and meekness."

Sloth—"in the wider sense is laziness and is opposed to diligence. In the narrower sense it means spiritual sloth.... It contradicts the virtues of piety and love of God."

In addition we have the seven main virtues: the theological ones—faith, hope and charity; the cardinal ones—prudence, justice, fortitude and temperance.[7]

Peschke notes that these lists are primarily "for spiritual incitement and ascetic reflections." They are, however, a part of the inherited wisdom on how to live as a Christian. It is easy to see how people could become judgmental about certain forbidden behaviour; all of life was meant to be covered by such guidelines.

Searchers may have difficulty labelling anything a "sin." They may say that cheating and lying, for example, are "wrong" and in some cases illegal, but they may see no reason for thinking of them as sins against a god—if there is one. This attitude is particularly prevalent in our society with regard to lust. We have a vast media system spewing out millions of items that encourage lust, and it appears to be the main preoccupation and pleasure of many people. There are even moralists who will argue that so long as no one is being hurt, fulfilling our lust is perfectly all right: our bodies were made to be enjoyed. However, it is instructive to look at what is happening to relationships between men and women. Since the advent of the birth control pill in the early 1960s, sex and its procreational function are more separate than ever before. It is my observation, however, that both men and women have been damaged by the emphasis on "sex for recreation." One of the tragic consequences is its contribution to the alarming rate of disintegration in families.

Sam Keen presents an interesting perspective on this in *Fire in the Belly*. He is dealing with the woundedness of men who were brought up to be warriors and are now condemned for the results. As he nears the end of his book, Keen turns to a consideration of how to bring about their healing:

> The only revolution that will heal us is one in which men and women come together and place the creation of a rich family life back in the center of the horizon of our values. A letter I got recently from a woman makes the point: "Perhaps the real shift will come when men fully realize, in the gut and not just in the head, that they are equally responsible, with women, for the creation, nurturing and protection of children—that children are not simple sex objects, ego trips, or nuisances, but their first responsibility—before war, money, power, and status."[8]

Individual acts have social consequences. Although theologians consistently argue that a person cannot be held accountable unless they realize what they are doing, Peschke notes that "members of a community [may be] guilty of an injustice into which they were drawn through their own choice or at least through their negligence or indifference."[9] Our behaviour in the areas of sexuality and respect for others, including children, and our choices of priorities have clearly resulted in suffering for many people. Searchers may not want to use the word "sin," but they recognize many situations as "not right" and may work diligently to try to eradicate or alleviate the suffering caused by the situation.

Forgiveness cannot enter a picture prior to an awareness of wrong having been committed. Forgiveness may be used comfortably by searchers if there are problems in their relationships with one another. But forgiveness may also be used by searchers who are arriving at a tentative faith in God. This is particularly important if the reason for the search is some tragedy or massive dislocation in an individual's life. A person may long for the ability to resolve and leave behind events that have happened. A broken relationship rarely occurs, for example, without harsh words and regrets.

In order to feel forgiven, Jesus emphasizes (in the Lord's Prayer) that we have to forgive. This involves recognition of both our own and others' responsibilities. Paul Tillich wrote: "The consciousness of guilt cannot be overcome by the simple assurance that man is forgiven," and "man can believe in forgiveness only if justice is maintained and guilt is confirmed."[10] In other words, forgiveness is not to be taken lightly. In fact, the experience of real confession and true forgiveness can lead searchers into the heart of the holy aspect of life, partly because it establishes a relationship of peace which we human beings long for. Moreover, confession and forgiveness bring about changes in the lives of both persons, helping them to understand the spiritual growth process. We are not "finished products" in the universe for as long as we live. We are "becoming" all the time. What we do and how we do it affects not only ourselves but others around us.

Searchers often dream of reaching a safe place where they can stop struggling and just enjoy life. There are moments of beautiful certainty in the Christian life—knowing that we are forgiven for the things we know we have done wrong offers us this reassurance. These beautiful moments can come quietly in a time of private prayer, or during a worship service. Or they can come after the weeping and wailing and gnashing of teeth when an individual has faced his or her own reality, alone or with a counsellor. The certainty that God is there, that God does forgive and welcome us "home" to the state we were made for may be a never-to-be-forgotten high. For such moments, Jesus lived and died. In such moments, no matter what our past experience has been, we know that we are whole persons worthy of loving care, with future possibilities we can gladly look forward to and which the world cannot take away.

Questions to Consider

1. What do you think of the word "sin"?
2. Have you ever felt forgiven in a way that really mattered?
3. Are any of the seven sins or virtues listed particularly meaningful to you?
4. Do you believe that God reaches out to you?

Experiencing Freedom, Sharing Love

O Jesus Christ grow thou in me,
and all things else recede;
my heart be daily nearer thee,
from sin be daily freed.
Fill me with gladness from above;
hold me by strength divine!
O let the glow of thy great love
thro' all my being shine.

Johann C. Lavater,
Songs for a Gospel People, #27

Douglas John Hall has written, "Sin, like its companion mystery, grace, cannot finally be understood; it can only be stood under, contemplated, and *confessed*."[11] Because partners are participating in a relationship, rather than primarily feeling called to obedience or searching for basic answers, they are the most likely among the three faithstyles to be able to enter into the meaning of both Lavater's hymn and Hall's statement. As in loving human relationships, there is wonder and joy at the same time as a tension of unknowing and unpredictability. We can experience times of almost miraculous closeness and times when, for reasons we may not understand, a distance develops. In the religious life, this distance may be caused by what theologians call sin, and it may be healed by forgiveness. It is a "making things right again" experience.

Thousands of books have been written about the role of Jesus in dealing with human sin. I have dealt briefly with some of the most common theories in the section on Jesus. I would like now to explore the particular vision of the crucifixion and the resurrection that partners may develop.

To begin our exploration, we must review the nature of the partner's relationship with God. In deep prayer or meditation, the partner feels united with God, Christ, the Spirit, our world, and the universe. This feeling of union is sensed rather than thought of separately, or abstractly. It is like the atmosphere all around us, rather than other persons or buildings. We enter another dimension of our human possibilities. God is not a person in the usual sense, but God can enter a personal relationship with us. All of our experience is well knit within this reality. We acknowledge the individual parts without destroying the whole.

Jesus said: "On that day you will know that I am in my Father, and you in me, and I in you" (John 14:20, NRSV). He is speaking to his disciples, reassuring them that, after his death, he will come again. "You will see me. Because I live, you also will live." The disciples did not understand this then and we do not fully understand now, but we know that what Jesus promised is true— there is new life, a different kind of reality available to us because of what he did. This is key to our Christian understanding of God and God's will as well as our understanding of who Jesus was and is.

As parents carry their children in their hearts, so God carries us in God's heart—if we may so speak. God wills a good life for us as parents will good lives for their children. God has tried throughout the course of history to guide us through laws and lessons. Yet we have still failed to grasp the point that God's love, not God's anger or desire to punish evil, is the major thrust of God's compassion for human beings. I know that some individuals have trouble with the idea of God being so "human," that feelings and changes in attitude are possible for God. However, the evidence of the Jesus event clearly demonstrates God's capacity for these. We must recognize that there is a great deal more to God than that which relates only to human beings: the Creator and the Sustainer of the whole universe obviously invokes different images of God's nature. The part that relates to human beings connects with the core, not the surface. It is a *spiritual* connection.

Throughout the ages, God found that only a few people were able to truly be in touch with God's Spirit. Thus, I dare to suggest that God thought, "I need to make it obvious in terms more people can understand. I need to be a real father to a real son. I need to *show* them, not just tell them, what my love is like." Therefore, Jesus came as a tiny, helpless baby in order to share the entire human experience from birth to death. We have many unanswered questions about what Jesus' life was really like before he turned up as a travelling teacher, preacher, and healer on the roads of the Holy Land.

The core of Jesus' ministry lies in his relationship with God— whom he called his father. A partner may very easily believe that her or his relationship with God is of the same nature as Jesus' was. This may sound blasphemous to some community faithstyle persons, but to me it makes sense. If Jesus was fully human, he did not have a "special track" connection to God. He lived out of the same awareness of divine guidance in his life that we can also know. His relationship with God grew close, and towards the end of his life, he saw that people were not going to be saved from their troubled lives solely by his teaching, or by the healing that he could do as a man. Remember Northrop Frye's words, which I quoted earlier: "Truths of the gospel kind cannot be demonstrated except through personal example." Jesus came to realize that *his* personal example was to give up his life in order to make his message about God come alive. He struggled and agonized about it, but he did it just the same. The world was permanently changed.

What did Jesus do? On the surface he literally gave up his life. He could easily have stayed out of Jerusalem, where he knew his enemies gathered, and lived to be an old man. He could have slipped out of Gethsemane and hidden in the hills until the danger had passed. But Jesus, with the loving guidance of God, stayed to face the enemy. He was subsequently killed by the brutal Roman method used to deal with lower-class criminals.

Many people chose to reject him, rather than change their way of thinking about God. We do not need to be told that this is still the case today. It is so easy for *us* to resist change!

What did Jesus do? On a deeper level, he showed how much God cares for us. God did not just come as a baby and, through a normal human life, establish a relationship with God. More important, God incarnate in the man Jesus faced the pain and evil with which humans have to struggle in the world. God, of course, was capable of doing something to prevent Jesus' death, but God did not perform any miracles. Parents who have "walked with" their children through hellish experiences can imagine what the cost was to God. One possible explanation is that God saw that humans could be helped by having to face two essential things: (*a*) how far away from God's will they are, and (*b*) that God is willing to take drastic action to help them to understand his loving purpose. Therefore, God was willing to experience human suffering and death![12]

"Were you there when they crucified my Lord?" is a beloved spiritual. I have seen people with tears streaming down their face as they heard or sang that hymn, because they really "were there." They had entered into the agony in a spiritual sense and had come out on the other side with their lives immensely changed. Throughout the ages, many denominations have emphasized the suffering of Jesus. I have heard of one minister who seems to "drip blood" in every sermon in order to stir up guilt in his congregation. He does not have an altar call or any other way of pronouncing a word of forgiveness. This seems to me to be a long way from what God intended! Yet, as I talk with people about their faith, I discover that this kind of influence was common in the "old days" and is still prevalent in some circles today.

The cross is to show God's love, not God's hate or anger. A partner shrinks from the kind of preaching or teaching that makes people feel less loved. This does not mean that a partner omits an assessment of his or her own spiritual state as the cross is contemplated. Partners recognize the need for confession and forgiveness, but this occurs within a loving context. If one's parents were excessively demanding and critical and never gave assurance of love, one may be emotionally unable to accept love as a whole person, even as a well-functioning adult. If one was abused as a child, comprehension of a "loving father God" may be impossible to grasp. The message of God's love being shown on the cross may be hard to grasp sometimes in light of one's past experience.

We are helped to understand God's love by hearing other people's stories of love breaking through. Christian writer and lecturer Keith Miller tells us his.

> I used to walk down the streets and suddenly break out in a cold sweat. I thought I might be losing my mind. One day it was so bad that I got in my company car and took off on a field trip alone. As I was driving through the tall pine woods country of East Texas I suddenly pulled up beside the road and stopped. I remember sitting there in complete despair....
>
> As I sat there I began to weep like a little boy, which I suddenly realized I was inside. I looked up toward the sky. There was nothing I wanted to do with my life. And I said, "God, if there's anything you want in this stinking soul, take it."
>
> This was almost ten years ago. But something came into my life that day which has never left. There wasn't any ringing of bells or flashing of lights or visions; but it was a deep intuitive realization of what it is God wants from a man, which I had never known before. And the peace which came with this understanding was not an experience in itself, but was rather a cessation of the conflict of a lifetime. I realized then that God does not want a man's

money, nor does He primarily want his time, even the whole lifetime of it a young seminarian is ready to give Him. God, I realized, doesn't want your time. He wants your *will*; and if you give Him your will, He'll begin to show you life as you've never seen it before.

It *is* like being born again. I saw that I had not seen Christ at Seminary because I had never known God personally.

As I sat there I continued to cry, only now the tears were a release from a lifetime of being bound by myself, by the terrific drive to prove that I am something—*what* I had never quite understood. Although I could not understand nor articulate for many months what had happened to me, I knew to the core of my soul that I had somehow made personal contact with the very Meaning of Life.[13]

This story reminds me of Jesus' saying that we have to decide who to follow. With so much confusion in our world, so many conflicting voices, it is not surprising that many people feel lost as Miller did. Many feel so burdened that they can hardly bear it. Yet the message of how people are helped by God has been so poorly handled in many churches that people hesitate to turn to church leaders as a likely source of help.

Partnership style persons could be more helpful to others in their congregation if they were more open about their faith. Because they are so frequently misunderstood, they may get into the habit of not speaking up at all. One reason they can be helpful is that they usually don't have preconceptions about how God will work with persons. There is no established pattern, as Miller reminds us. He felt that he had "made contact with the very Meaning of Life." Others may feel close to Jesus or God in a specific way. Monica Furlong describes one of her transcendental experiences: "… although no word had been uttered, I felt myself spoken to. I was aware of being regarded by love, of being wholly accepted, accused, forgiven, all at once. The joy of it was the greatest I had ever known in my life. I felt I had been born for this moment and had marked time till it occurred." Furlong reports that she "went to church, received Communion, argued with the priest.... The priest affected me as much as anyone has done in my life. He was nervous of me, unwilling to say much, locked in his own depressive problems. Yet he was also joyful— he shone with a love and with a care for me which was irresistible."[14] If only everyone who has such spiritual experiences were so fortunate!

The pattern of partnership style forgiveness has been illustrated in these stories from Miller and Furlong. It is not so much a transaction as an event. Whatever sins or misdirections have occurred are swallowed up in the holy fire of the experience. The whole person is changed. On an everyday level, the partner will often confess and feel forgiven in less spectacular ways—but the base is still the same, rooted in God's loving acceptance and desire for better things to come. Words like anger and punishment are not appropriate, but firmness and justice are. Partners know that they are accountable both to God and to those with whom they worship and live in community.

Finally, we need to reconsider the resurrection experience. It is a new beginning. For Jesus, the human body is left behind. The new body is spiritual, and consequently, the new work is spiritual. Our hymns celebrate the resurrection victory over death and sin. The resurrected Jesus is the sign of God's working with humans in a new way. The written Law has been superseded by the internal Spirit. Out of human weakness and death comes the transformation of life.

I have a particular fondness for the image of the resurrection because, in a human way, I experienced one. After many years of weakness and pain, when my heart often prevented me from even walking across my apartment and on one occasion simply stopped, a new medicine and an inexplicable change in my immune system made it possible for me to return to work part time. I felt a joy too wonderful for words. Some of my most meaningful experiences in ministry have occurred since that time. My experience of weakness opened a whole new area in my life. I had always pushed myself despite pain and exhaustion, feeling that I had to do things that were expected of me to be acceptable to others. Now I respect my body and its needs, and I have a new base for my sense of self. As I spend more and more time on spirituality, I find not only new strength but a new direction. Life is very different from before.

In closing this chapter, I want to return to God's being with Jesus through the death experience, instead of God as the harsh father ordering the pain, the traditional image of the cross' work. I want to address particularly those people who had harsh parents and say to them, as forcefully as I can, that the Bible is right when it says "God is love." God's love was strong enough to hang on a cross in the heat of the day with a beloved human being. God's love is also strong enough to be with us through our worst pain and nightmares. Yes, we sin. Yes, we need to confess our sins. Yes, we need forgiveness. Yes, forgiveness is freely offered. No, we are not miserable wretches worthy only of misery and punishment. We are not intended to live life in fear and trembling of doing something wrong. Rather, we are invited to enjoy life in an atmosphere of acceptance and guidance as we share in God's good intentions for us and our world. We are called to be partners: to carry on the work of Jesus in our world. We are not alone. We are never alone. We only think we are when we reject the love God so freely offers.

I close this section with a prayer from my daily devotional book, *Disciplines*:

Create in us anew, O Lord, a sense of awe and excitement and urgency as we realize the privilege that is ours to share the best news ever to be communicated on planet Earth.

Let the power of the message transform us and, through us, touch the world you love. In Jesus' name. Amen.[15]

Questions to Consider

1. Does your life have a meaning?
2. What do you remember being taught about the cross?
3. Is it hard to forgive? To accept forgiveness?
4. If you could ask God for anything and knew that you would receive just what you asked for, what would it be?

III

WORKING WITH THE FAITHSTYLES

Chapter Ten

The Common Ground of Mainline Churches

A new church is trying to be born ... but most of us aren't even in the throes of labour yet.

Donna Schaper,
A Book of Common Power, 96[1]

The first section of this book introduces faithstyles. The second section shows how they may be experienced. Now I will explore how they may work in practical situations.

Every life, and therefore every form of faith, is lived within a context. There are influences from the past and the present that determine what people are able to believe is possible. These influences may affect whether persons care about maintaining or developing anything related to the faith they have known in the past. Attendance, for example, has become a major problem in mainline churches, yet there are many new styles of faith being successfully promoted. Congregations need to assess whether they are dealing with the realities of the people around them. This means becoming more objective about what *could* be done to provide more people with what they need to enjoy or grow.

For many congregations, questions such as, "How can people

who have radically different beliefs about God worship in the same church service?" or "Is it possible for a searcher to do a complete search in a familiar congregation?" are urgent. We live together with others in many different circumstances—from homes to dormitories to shared apartments to our own family houses to retirement homes. Sometimes we care deeply for the people who share space with us, and sometimes we hardly know them. We have laws based on respect for the rights of others, including the practice of faith. Yet in many faith communities, the most troublesome problems come from attitudes towards customary practices in worship or leadership styles. Familiar hymns, for example, are extremely important to some people, while boring others into absenteeism.

In this chapter, we are going to look at some of the common ground on which these matters have to be handled. In the next chapter, we will look beyond the common ground to a future which is even now in process, but not at all entirely clear. Both situations challenge us to look with openness and courage towards a fresh way of living the faith.

The following quotation came from Patricia Hopkins' "inner voice" when she was trying to keep herself awake to prolong a pleasant meditation: "You always think the way to God involves overpowering the natural. You think it means forcing and suffering. Haven't you learned yet that loving God is as natural and nurturing as sleep? Why do you insist on making it hard?"[2] She and Sherry Ruth Anderson interviewed around two hundred women about their spiritual lives, and were beginning to work on a book about their findings. They "had begun to think of development as some achievement like the development of pectoral muscles or shopping centers." Without struggle the seeker would find "there is nothing to attain in the first place." Yet the teaching is clear that "the end state cannot be 'gotten', that it comes in its own time or through grace."[3] By the time they finished their interviews, the women felt certain that spiritual growth arises from an inner reality rather than an external rule book. It is a gift rather than a prize for good behaviour, yet the path of progress does contain elements of upheaval and struggle.

As I think of the concrete realities within which people have been and are being shaped today, I realize why our mainline churches are in such trouble. Institutions such as churches move slowly, even when change in society is occurring rapidly. Our churches are products of the conditioning process of a society and a world drastically different from the society and world of today. "If you study hard and get a good job and behave yourself, you're set for life" is the advice my 1950s university classmates received. Women were heartily encouraged to look for men with good prospects, so life would be good for their children. There was a deep sense of security in feeling that "God's in His heaven, all's right with the world."

That feeling is gone now for vast numbers of people. For rural folk, it is linked to the instability of their livelihood in farming or fishing. Many employees who thought they had their whole working lives "sewn up" are now walking the streets looking for any job to provide food for their family. From some of those with great riches comes a public admission that they have lost everything they built so eagerly, not that many years ago. All around us is tremendous loss, accompanied by tremendous amounts of grief and pain.

Our mainline churches have tended to take two paths: doing practical things, such as organizing food banks and putting pressure on governmental authorities; and encouraging people to follow the established paths of spiritual discipline to endure the hardship. It is rare for a mainline church to give leadership to the kind of exploration Hopkins was engaged in, because the work challenges the base of the received traditional faith. The premise of the exploration was that God may be working on something unfamiliar and we had better begin to get acquainted with it. If a new church is trying to be born, as Schaper tells us, we need to look for signs and decide how we might assist the process of labour.

All three faithstyles assume that people are open to communication with God. The majority of people like familiar ways of communicating. They like to "know where they are" in any situation and what they can reasonably expect. If a system was being designed to frustrate and frighten, a designer could not do better than the turmoil of today. People often say things like, "We don't know where to turn" and "Why would God do such a thing to us?" This is hard to face, frightening to consider, and may, furthermore, block healthy thinking of solutions.

Alfred North Whitehead puts the matter into perspective for us:

> Our sociological theories, our political philosophy, our practical maxims of business, our political economy, and our doctrines of education are derived from an unbroken tradition of great thinkers and of practical examples, from the age of Plato in the fifth century before Christ to the end of the last century. The whole of this tradition is warped by the vicious assumption that each generation will substantially live amid the conditions governing the lives of its fathers and will transmit those conditions to mold with equal force the lives of its children. We are living in the first period of human history for which this assumption is false.[4]

Whitehead's perspective assures us that we are not overreacting to the massive changes that confront us. These changes give us no clues as to what the future may bring. This is common human ground. Television allows us to see and hear peoples who were once foreign to us as they seek to cope with their own changing situations. We now know that unlimited "growth" will not increase our chances for a good life. We know that one part of the world's population cannot ignore the plights of other parts. We know through scientific means that we can destroy our environment. We are forced to think of others and other circumstances when many individuals still have trouble with a "strange" family moving into their neighbourhood. These are tough realities to face. They challenge the very basis of our lives as well as our faith.

I have noticed that the following five reactions to change are especially common and have noted some faithstyle responses:

1. Long for the past. Idealize it. Romanticize it. Forget its problems. Use it to judge everything in the present. Do not grieve and get it over with. Resist every effort to make the best of the present. The people most dependent on their traditions will find it hardest to handle change. They may, in fact, feel that their very lives are threatened. They need a lot of support.

2. Never get away from the pressure. Feel constantly burdened, unable to think clearly, afraid of everything. Often results in headaches, stomach trouble, family fights, heart disease, high blood pressure. This is an easy road to disaster, if the individual does not try to perceive reality clearly and take some steps to deal with it. Even a small step that gives some control over the situation back to the individual will let steam out of the pressure-cooker quality of such a life. Learning to detach in meditation, as partners are particularly likely to do, gives the body and mind a rest while allowing one's inner spirit to receive help and guidance.

3. Get angry at everyone and everything that is involved in the predicament. Anger is a two-edged sword: it can be used to attack a real problem or it can be turned destructively inward. Just to repeat a list of complaints without taking action is hurtful to a person and leads to despair. However, anger that is soundly based and understood can bring about significant advances for a distressed person. It is helpful to look at anger carefully—it may have a message in it about possible action.

Talking the matter through with God can often give a healthy perspective on the problem.

4. Give in. Admit you're "licked." Just endure as best you can. Those who believe that they deserve punishment because they were greedy, or otherwise at fault, often react this way to change. Their pain is made holy in their feelings. Their hope is that God will forgive them and allow things to straighten out so that a good life will still be possible. This position gives the least hope of renewed energy for whatever life brings, because it casts people as helpless victims. There are many passages in the Bible that reinforce the idea that the good are rewarded by prosperity and the evil are punished by trouble. The Bible also has many passages that promise forgiveness, but they may slide out of the consciousness of troubled individuals, especially those with a strong traditional faith base.

It is important to note that many people feel powerless now because they are, in fact, controlled to a great extent by powerful commercial, political, and social institutions. The temptation to simply give up their familiar way of life is very great, and it may at times be the best choice possible. It matters, however, whether a person realizes that they have the freedom to choose—even if the choices are desperately hard. To feel powerless and manipulated by others destroys one's sense of being worthwhile.

Community faithstyle persons are the most likely to feel that they must accept what God gives; searchers are most likely to seek a new meaning in the new situation. However, no one can really predict how anyone will react as his or her life is forced into change.

5. Finally, some people are able to mix suffering with trust that there is meaning to be found even in pain. Hope, then, can be born amid the ashes of former security. Like the exiles in Babylon long ago, people can often find new possibilities. Those who are able to take this approach find life more

manageable. They dream more realistic dreams. They allow their energy to develop at its own rate instead of frantically trying to force new ways. They are frequently the same people who talk about their problems with others. Through giving and receiving emotional support and exchanging ideas, they can find more possibilities and hope. One of the important contributions of a church focused on faithstyles is that those involved in it learn to accept differing attitudes without fear or lack of respect. As a result, communication is much more likely to occur and to be valued.

My work on faithstyles began as a result of my being confronted, while a rural pastor, with an enormous amount of pain. This pain turned up in many guises. In the early 1980s, it was easy to have faith that the problems of high interest rates and the "dip" in the economy were only passing nightmares. The struggle with the realities of the following years made me well acquainted with all of the above reaction styles. Although I had been trained in both theology and pastoral counselling, I realized that we did not have the necessary tools with which to connect to the deeper levels of faith in this difficult time.

When I encountered the characteristic belief that "God must be doing this for some reason," I had to battle internally with whether it was better to introduce the idea of another way of "looking at" or "believing in" God, or better to use the faith that had formerly sustained people. Make no mistake about this: the community faithstyle has proven itself to be enormously helpful to countless people, in all types of trouble, over the course of many centuries. The trust that some persons have in God is so beautiful—and so deep—that no one would want to damage it in any way. I found myself longing for a way to present possibilities without judgement or pressure, so that everyone would enjoy more freedom within the faith community.

A striking example of this need for freedom came when I

visited a woman who had lost a member of her family to a long, drawn-out battle with cancer. She had abandoned the accepted words and patterns; neighbours thought she had lost her faith. To me, she said, "But my faith is much stronger than it has ever been. I just have a different way of understanding how God works with people." Then she told me sadly that she could no longer attend worship: "The words are all wrong for me now," and "Others look at me as if I have become a heretic." Somewhat later I met another startling gap in congregational acceptance: an older woman visited a gospel mission in another town and was "saved." Everyone immediately assumed that she would shift her membership to the mission, which meant someone driving several miles to pick her up and then take her home. When I visited and asked her if she had considered staying with our congregation, she said, "Oh no! They wouldn't understand. I took Christ as my Saviour. I have to be with others who will help me grow." I was sad to discover that her neighbours were relieved to be free of such a "Jesus person."

I gradually came to understand how limited many of our church practices and words can be. You may fit in a mainline church like you fit into a country club—you like the hours, the space, the opportunities given, the shared values of the members, the costs, and the "contacts." Where, I began to ponder, did faith enter this picture? I came to the reluctant conclusion that it was not faith but established practice that mattered most to many people. If you didn't like it, you could go elsewhere, and that attitude is, of course, the basic reason for our empty pews today. People of all faithstyles will no longer sit still for irrelevance if they are looking for spiritual nourishment. They are not content with having to dig for it or ignore many practices in their accustomed place of worship. They want their style of approaching faith acknowledged as a natural part of the relationship of God and persons. They can then feel included and valued.

There are some particular problems in many of our mainline

churches that stem from theological schools. The school's agendas are so heavy that it is sometimes mistakenly thought that a private devotional life is a student's personal business and not that of the school. As a result, a survey in one prestigious American divinity school revealed that "over two thirds of these students stated they did not pray at all on any regular basis."[5] Since questions about prayer are frequently asked early in a person's search for a closer relationship with God, this is a startling and disheartening fact indeed.

Theological graduates of my era were strongly conditioned to preach the gospel and to help people grow in faith. The power of the gospel was an awesome and wonderful energy in our thinking and feeling. Congregational members expected to be able to share faith experiences within a common frame of reference. Visits to homes strengthened bonds of friendship. It is true that pastors were "set apart" and in some cases abused the authority that many people wanted them to exercise. In general, however, those in paid, accountable ministry were in close touch with the lives of the members of their congregations.

There are a host of reasons why this picture has changed. The issue of visiting is one example. Career and other interests make it difficult for members to find the time to receive the pastor. Baby Boomers often see the church as there to meet their needs on demand, rather than as a partner in a sustained relationship. They appreciate a pastor who is a competent counsellor, for example, but do not think of him or her as a friend unless they themselves are involved in other areas of the church's life. Many younger people have mixed feelings about both the clergy and the "powers that be" in a church. Understanding faithstyles makes it easier to deal with the variety of needs that must be addressed.

Clergy are now being taught to respect their own needs and the resulting behaviour disturbs many community faithstyle persons who look for "unselfish" ministers, always on call to help in any possible way. This attitude fostered many unreasonable expectations, leading to stress and breakdowns for pastors. We are now in the process of demanding that clergy become less parental, and members of the congregation, more powerful. This leads, in many cases, to new kinds of strife, partly because there is no longer general acceptance of set beliefs about what a Christian should be like, and what she or he should do.

It is therefore extremely important that the centre of faith, spiritual experience, be recovered as a focal point. We have seen how faith can be expressed in a variety of ways. If we are going to improve the prospects for our mainline churches, we had better face the reality that people come to church when it is a place that helps them to grow in *their* faith—from where they are. The only way we can be satisfactory ministers, priests, rabbis, or pastors these days is to learn from talking and sharing with people about what interests them in the area of faith and what they would like to do about it.

This book was born out of a strong need to help people understand that ministry begins with persons. We need to be clearer about the options each person has to develop as God guides them. Our role is to keep doors open and encourage reflection, searching, and sharing. We can do all of these things from our base in the common ground of faith, but we need to be aware of the possibilities and be willing to take some risks.

Questions to Consider

1. Do you agree with any of the material in this chapter? Why?
2. Do you disagree with any of the material in this chapter? Why?
3. If someone asks you a question you cannot answer, how do you feel? What do you do about it?
4. If you get into a conversation with someone who seems to be really close with God, how do you feel? What do you do about it?
5. What kind of conversation about faith makes you entirely comfortable?

Chapter Eleven

Living Together in Active Faith

*Lord, help us to be patient with new Christians who
seem to have lost their perspective as they entered a
new relationship with You. If they become temporarily
blinded to the ordinary responsibilities and old friends
around them, help us to provide an atmosphere in
which this new relationship with You can be tested
and translated into deeper relationships with people.
Help us in the church to let new Christians enjoy the
excitement of discovery without our hypercritical
judgment—even though there may be some anxious
moments about their soundness and responsibility.*

Keith Miller,
Habitation of Dragons[1]

*If the assumption is made that the congregation is a
flowing, living, growing, expanding organism, then
present limitations can be viewed as relative not
absolute boundaries.*

Denham Grierson,
Transforming a People of God[2]

These two quotations sound a warning bell! This chapter is going to be about change at the centre of personal and congregational life and it will not likely be comforting to those who want their faith to be like a beautiful mohair blanket wrapped around them. To others, it may be a breath of fresh air.

Keith Miller wrote about individuals who have had an experience of meeting Christ at a gathering where feelings were deeply stirred, who have had their lives change suddenly and dramatically. Denham Grierson wrote about becoming part of "A People of God" through the way members of a congregation associate with one another. These are only two ways out of countless possibilities to change one's religious life—one is personal, quick, and dramatic; the other is communal, gradual, and not always recognized. Both authors, however, make it clear that such events are not isolated. Other people are affected— and they affect the way in which the new experience may be understood and become effective.

We need to be clear that there is a tremendous difference between learning the words and ideas of the faith and experiencing faith as an in-depth part of a whole person. The first is based in the brain; the second, in the essential core of one's whole being. It has been the traditional practice of mainline churches to load the brain with all the history and doctrine of the particular denomination and expect "good Christians" to result. Meanwhile, other denominations have simultaneously stressed experiences of the "heart."

I am more and more convinced that neither approach is the most satisfactory way to proceed. I believe that persons are *whole*, not bits and pieces. God does not address our brain, or our feelings, as if they were independent entities. Here is a report from a prayer group:

From the beginning, we have accepted the fact that while we participate in the mystery, we cannot know it. Yet from this very "not knowing" has come some of our greatest gifts. For in the silence we feel free to voice our doubts and questions when they arise, to just be with them without seeking absolute answers. And as a result we are learning, as Rilke suggested, to "love the questions themselves. Although we do not always know the way to God, our collective heart reminds us again and again as we sit together in the silence that God knows the way to us."[3]

For those persons who always want a clear and immediate answer, such experiences would not be helpful. However, for those who are struggling, who are trying to figure things out, who are seeking to find a way to maintain their own values, such experiences are precious beyond words. There are large numbers of people in our society who would never think of accepting the whole doctrinal position of an established church but who seek out group situations of freedom combined with support in which they are encouraged to move with more confidence through their life. They are *hungry* for such affirmation of their being and God's living presence.

Living together in congregations can provide the same sort of acceptance—or not. I remember a church choir member talking about how frustrating it was to her to be valued only as a singer. "Doesn't anybody care about *me?*" she asked. "I'm a person. I'm not just a voice. Why doesn't someone talk with *me?*" In small congregations especially, very heavy demands may be made on both men and women to do whatever needs to be done, regardless of their wishes. Many church members are well-trained in "duty"!

Young people frequently have startling ideas that require a lot of time and energy. Older people may say, "It's not practical. They'll never get it done," and sit back to watch what happens. Yet if they entered into it with enthusiasm and did what they could, not only would the whole project be easier, but everyone would feel a whole lot better.

I have recently become aware of a troubling and exaggerated attitude towards men's spirituality while women's spirituality is being brought to the fore. My experience has been that men are engaged as frequently as women in both learning and experiencing their faith. I remember one male searcher in particular who provided excellent commentary on my sermons and often provoked growth in my understanding.

It is true that men frequently see things from a different perspective than women. However, both sexes have been damaged by society's emphasis on their respective qualities. It is sometimes easier to accept women's "soft" gifts and special connection to nature than it is to accept men's "hard" gifts and their drive to "get ahead." Many people now do not like competitiveness and "wildman" qualities. In a church based on faithstyle acceptance, these troubling splits could be eased by acceptance of persons as whole. Then the "hard" qualities in women and the "soft" qualities in men could be acknowledged without question. All people, no matter where they are in their understanding of God and themselves, would be welcome to explore, experiment, share, and enjoy a relationship with energy and acceptance in it.

One of the most common problems in our churches is persons who hold positions of power and cannot or will not change. Their faith may have stopped developing when they joined the church at age twelve or so. All the old forms may have become sacred to them. The problem may be to accept the contribution of these persons as equally important as the rest of the congregation and to give their faith needs equal consideration. This means, for example, that old hymns are sometimes sung, but new ones may also be introduced. It means inclusive language might be used wisely and generally but occasionally the KJV, especially the Psalms and the Holy Season readings, might be used as well. Tolerance of the different faithstyles may be all that can be achieved but it is better than open conflict and an empty or abandoned church. A friendly tolerance often eases tension and decreases confrontation. It is also wise to remember that such key persons often have knowledge that can be very useful to the whole congregation. If such a person feels valued as a person he or she will be more willing and able to be co-operative.

One of the most interesting and satisfying things about a faithstyle-based church is working with people who are growing in faith. In *Living the Faith Community*, John Westerhoff III draws a detailed picture of this possibility. Using classical structures of the church year and sacraments, Westerhoff shows how faith is formed in a healthy community where people of all kinds and ages are respected and the shared life is focused on God's loving purpose for all.[4] The congregation would not be alarmed when a new Christian lost his or her perspective or sense of responsibility, which Keith Miller refers to in the opening quotation, but would provide a steady balance. "Being there for you" is a popular way of phrasing what a support person does for people in transition. A faithstyle church would always have people ready to "be there" for those in need. It is the very opposite of the cold, judgmental quality often found in churches today that insist on trying to carry on in the old way. The focus of church life shifts from surviving to celebrating the realities of what God is doing with the lives of all involved.

In one of my Project on Rural Ministry Network Newsletters, I listed the following eight characteristics of a faith-centred ministry:

1. It focuses on the individual *as the base* for congregational life.
2. It assumes that faith changes throughout life so that two needs are constant: affirmation of the tradition presently accepted and encouragement of the "growing edges."
3. The risk in seeking out and working with searchers must be taken.

4. Partnership persons should be given roles that are appropriate to their gifts.
5. The change in community faithstyle assumptions centres on a change in attitude towards tradition. For example, "We have always got through in the past" translates to "We *can* meet the needs of the present and future."
6. The current needs have to be identified and accepted, as much as possible, by the whole congregation.
7. Individuals are accepted as part of the faith community on the basis of their willingness to take part in its activities. Assent to doctrine may lead to formal membership, which is seen as a beginning rather than an ending. As with families, growth and development is for all interested persons.
8. Clergy or leader persons need to: be very secure in their own faith, so that the doubt and struggles of others do not personally threaten them; have a strong theological base—including traditional as well as modern formulations; have some skills in spiritual direction and group dynamics; and have no need to dominate *or* be subservient in relationships.

I have given the above examples to encourage readers to think through the situations in their life and/or religious centre that cause disagreement. In small communities, people often refrain from mentioning the things that are bothering them, because they fear ostracism or an open fight. Sometimes, there is a clear leader whose word is law and who effectively shuts people up. Disagreement itself may be frightening, but when it is accompanied by anger, it is absolutely terrifying to many people. So in a community of any faithstyle, where any one person or small group makes decisions unilaterally, the Spirit is frustrated. I know that getting everyone to agree may be impossible, but it is not impossible for everyone to be heard and respected. This is particularly important if different faithstyles are involved.

One of the most common disagreements is about obedience to tradition or Bible. It is impossible to predict who may want to "obey" and who may want to do something else. Persons in all three faithstyles have moments of rebellion or questioning. In some areas, there is a thrust from the fundamentalist wing of the Christian Church that is making us sharply aware of the differences between the traditional community faithstyle and fundamentalism. The latter, of course, is much more concerned about faithfulness to the Bible and also emphasizes "faith in the heart." The fear of loss of control of the community faithstyle contrasts with the fundamentalist desire to be under the control of the Spirit. For the fundamentalist, obedience to the Bible is assumed.

I have attempted to encourage people to exercise more freedom without losing either a sense of the God of history and theology or the God who meets us in the Spirit. I have tried to make clear that changes in the way we connect with God's Grace can be made without destroying a previous traditional base or the free explorations of one's mind. The best environment for a Christian who wishes to grow with such freedom is a place where tradition is honoured, where people who ask questions are welcomed as active participants, and everyone is willing to share at least some of their own spiritual journey. This environment clearly does not limit one's concerns to one institution; it opens up the whole area of God's activity in us, each other, and the world. It is an infinitely more exciting place when people take living their faith together seriously, care about one another, share and know the feeling of being part of a living, growing organism. The possibility exists for us all! We may all pray and sing together:

Help us accept each other as Christ accepted us;
teach us as sister, brother, each person to embrace.
Be present, God, among us and bring us to believe
we are ourselves accepted and meant to love and live.

Teach us, O God, your lessons, as in our daily life
we struggle to be human and search for hope and faith.
Teach us to care for people, for all—not just for some,
to love them as we find them or as they may become.
Let your acceptance change us, so that we may be moved
in living situations to do the truth in love;
to practise your acceptance until we know by heart
the table of forgiveness and laughter's healing art.

Lord, for today's encounters with all who are in need,
who hunger for acceptance, for righteousness and bread,
we need new eyes for seeing, new hands for holding on:
renew us with your Spirit; come, free us, make us one![5]

Questions to Consider

1. Would you like the feeling of being linked to a mystery?
2. Who or what do you find irritating or unhelpful in your present faith practices?
3. What fills you with joy and anticipation?
4. Are there some immediate ways in which you could make your life and your faith more compatible with that of others?

Notes

Introduction

1. James W. Fowler, *Stages of Faith: The Psychology of Human Development and the Quest for Meaning* (San Francisco: Harper & Row, 1981), 118-211.
2. John H. Westerhoff III and William H. Willimon, *Liturgy and Learning through the Life Cycle* (New York: Seabury Press, 1980), 77.
3. M. Scott Peck, *The Road Less Traveled* (New York: Simon & Schuster, 1978); *The Different Drum* (New York: Simon & Schuster, 1987), 188.
4. Peck, *The Different Drum*, 195.

Part I

Chapter One: The Community Faithstyle

1. Carl S. Dudley, *Unique Dynamics of the Small Church* (Washington: The Alban Institute, Inc., 1977).
2. Carol Gilligan, *In A Different Voice* (Cambridge, Mass.: Harvard University Press, 1982). Gilligan describes how women may make decisions based on the needs of important people in their lives. It seems to me to be a question of degree of knowledge and/or involvement rather than gender, at least in some cases.

Chapter Two: The Searcher Faithstyle

1. Fowler's *Stages of Faith* contains reports on his basic research and presents a clear argument for growth in faith being related to growth in other areas of life. His later book, *Faith Development and Pastoral Care* (Philadelphia: Fortress Press, 1987), is extremely helpful in understanding the consequences for congregations when faith development is taken seriously.
2. Westerhoff and Willimon, 77.
3. Ibid.
4. Peck, *The Different Drum*, 199.
5. Alex R. Sim, *Land and Community: Crisis in Canada's Countryside* (Guelph: Guelph University Press, 1988), 103ff.
6. Ibid., 107.
7. Ibid., 131.

Chapter Three: The Partnership Faithstyle

1. Peck, *The Different Drum*, 199.
2. Blaise Pascal, "Fire at Night," in *Pensées* (New York: E.P. Dutton & Co., 1966), 309.
3. Ollie Miller, *Sowing Circles of Hope* (Toronto: Women's Inter-Church Council of Canada,1990).
4. Piri Thomas, "I Asked the Big Man," in *Down These Mean Streets* (New York: Alfred A. Knopf, 1967), 316-317.

Part II

Chapter Four: God

1. Fowler, *Faith Development and Pastoral Care*, 41.
2. Leslie F. Brandt, *Psalms Now* (St. Louis: Concordia, 1973), 160-161.
3. Francis Thompson, "The Hound of Heaven," in Louis Untermeyer, ed., *A Treasury of Great Poems* (New York: Simon & Schuster, 1942), 1002-1006.
4. Fowler, *Faith Development and Pastoral Care*, 34-35. Fowler's use of the term "partnership" for this stage of faith development was not familiar to me until very recently. I had coined the term for my own use in 1986. Fowler's theological development of this theme is enormously helpful for many reasons but, in this context, I found it gives a *reason for being* to small and rural churches.
5. Daniel Day Williams, *The Spirit and the Forms of Love* (New York: Harper & Row, 1968), 12-13.
6. James K. Manley, "Spirit, Spirit of gentleness," in *Songs for a Gospel People* (Winfield, B.C.: Wood Lake Books, 1987), #108.

Chapter Five: Creation

1. Archibald MacLeish, *Riders on the Earth* (Boston: Houghton Mifflin Co., 1978), xiv.
2. Walter Brueggemann, "Land: Fertility and Justice," in Evans and Cusack, eds., *Theology of the Land* (Collegeville, Minn.: The Liturgical Press, 1987), 43.
3. Charles M. Wood, "The Question of the Doctrine of Providence," in *Theology Today* (July 1992): 210.
4. *The Heidelberg Catechism*, trans. Allen O. Miller and M. Eugene Osterhaven (Philadelphia: United Church Press, 1962). The comment about ecumenicity is by the translators. Cited by Wood, 209.
5. Wood, 224.
6. Verna Ross McGiffin, *In Search of Wisdom* (Winfield, B.C.: Wood Lake Books, 1990), 83.
7. William Wordsworth, *Lines Composed above Tintern Abbey*, in Untermeyer, 640.
8. Matthew Fox, *A Spirituality Named Compassion* (San Francisco: Harper & Row, 1979), 36-37.

9. Matthew Fox, *Original Blessing* (Santa Fe, N.M.: Bear and Company, 1983), 205.
10. Fox, *Original Blessing*, 206.
11. McGiffin, 89.
12. Sam Keen, *Fire in the Belly: On Being a Man* (New York: Bantam Books, 1991), 232.
13. Ibid., 224.
14. McGiffin, 67.

Chapter Six: Jesus

1. E. K. Emurian, *Living Stories of Famous Hymns* (Grand Rapids: Baker Book House, 1955), 138.
2. Northrop Frye, *The Double Vision* (Toronto: The United Church Publishing House, 1991), 20.
3. Ibid., 21.
4. *Reader's Digest* (June 1992), 117. Condensed from *Newsweek*, January 6, 1992.
5. William Johnston, ed., *The Cloud of Unknowing and the Book of Privy Counseling* (Garden City, N.Y.: Image Books, 1973), 52.
6. Lawrence LeShan, *How To Meditate* (Boston: Little, Brown and Company, 1974), 49.
7. Sister Mary, ODC, ed., *Living Water: Daily Readings with St. Teresa of Avila* (London: Darton, Longman and Todd, 1985), 42-43.
8. Douglas John Hall, *God and Human Suffering* (Minneapolis: Augsburg, 1986), 137.
9. Fowler, *Faith Development and Pastoral Care*, 97, 98.
10. Hall, 142.
11. Teilhard de Chardin, in Mark Link S.J., ed., *Take Off Your Shoes* (Niles, Ill.: Argus Communications, 1972), 64.

Chapter Seven: The Bible

1. Words: Wm. W. How, 1867, rev. Music: *Neuvermehrtes Gesang Buch*, 1963, rev. From *Songs for a Gospel People*.
2. *Statement of Faith* was prepared by the Committee on Christian Faith and authorized by the ninth General Council (1940) of The United Church of Canada. Published by the Division of Mission in Canada.
3. R. Theodore Lutz, "The Authority of the Bible" (Paper presented to London Conference on President's Day, London, Ontario, March 22, 1988).
4. Paul J. Achtemeier, ed., *Harper's Bible Dictionary* (San Francisco: Harper & Row, 1985), 193.
5. Herbert O'Driscoll, "A Certain Life," in *Contemporary Meditations on the Way of Christ* (Toronto: The Anglican Book Centre, 1980); Albert Schweitzer, *The Psychiatric Study of Jesus* (Boston: Beacon, 1948); Anthony Burgess, *Man of Nazareth* (New York: Bantam Books, 1979).
6. Brandt, 53.
7. Fowler, *Faith Development and Pastoral Care*, 120.

Chapter Eight: The Holy Spirit

1. This hymn is also in *The Hymnary* (Toronto: The United Church Publishing House, 1930), #157. There is a change of one line in v. 1: "stoop to my weakness, mighty as Thou art" is *The Hymnary* wording.
2. Claude Brown, "Trying to 'be good,'" in Louis M. Savary, ed., *Listen to Love* (New York: Regina Press, 1968), 185.
3. John Donne, "All times are his seasons," in Savary, 347.
4. Teilhard de Chardin, *The Divine Milieu*, trans. Bernard Wall (New York: Harper & Row, 1960), 78.
5. Teilhard de Chardin, in Link, *Take Off Your Shoes*, 41.
6. William James, *The Varieties of Religious Experience: A Study in Human Nature* (New York: New American Library, Inc., 1958), 367.
7. Abraham H. Maslow, *Religions, Values, and Peak-Experiences* (West Lafayette, Ind.: Kappa Delta Pi, 1970), 20.
8. Ibid., 24-25.
9. Ibid, x.
10. Hall, 131.
11. Dag Hammarskjold, *Markings* (New York: Alfred A. Knopf, 1964), 13.
12. Hall, 133.
13. Hammarskjold, 89.

Chapter Nine: Sin and Forgiveness

1. Achtemeier, 955.
2. *The United Church of Canada Service Book* (Toronto: The Ryerson Press, 1969), 15.
3. The Working Unit on Worship and Liturgy, *A Sunday Liturgy: For Optional Use in The United Church of Canada* (Toronto: The United Church of Canada, 1984), 7, 8.
4. Keith Miller, *The Taste of New Wine* (Waco, Texas: Word Books, 1965), 55.
5. Hall, 57.
6. Frye, 4.
7. Karl H. Peschke, *Christian Ethics* (Alcester, England: C. Goodliffe Neale, 1993), I, 306.
8. Keen, 226.
9. Peschke, 287.
10. Paul Tillich, *Systematic Theology* (Chicago: University of Chicago Press, 1951), I, 288.
11. Hall, 89.
12. I am indebted to Douglas John Hall for some of the ideas here. In his book *God and Human Suffering*, he argues powerfully in the chapter on redemption that God identifies with humanity (p. 108) and has entered effectively and without reserve into the life of the world (p. 109).
13. Miller, 32-33.
14. Monica Furlong, *Travelling In* (Cowley Publications, 1984), 27.
15. Joe A. Harding in *The Upper Room Disciplines* (Nashville: Upper Room Books, 1992), 140.

Part III

Chapter Ten: The Common Ground of Mainline Churches

1. Donna Schaper, *A Book of Common Power* (San Diego: Lura Media, 1989), 96.
2. Sherry Ruth Anderson and Patricia Hopkins, *The Feminine Face of God* (New York: Bantam Books, 1991), 119.
3. Ibid., 120.
4. Alfred North Whitehead, "An Assumption," in Savary and O'Connor eds., *The Heart Has Its Seasons* (New York: Regina Press, 1971), 31.
5. Anderson and Hopkins, 125. It is also reported that "over 80% of the class responded negatively" to the question: "Have you ever had a deep experience of prayer?"

Chapter Eleven: Living Together in Active Faith

1. Keith Miller, *Habitation of Dragons* (New York: Pillar Books, 1970), 136.
2. Denham Grierson, *Transforming a People of God* (Melbourne: Joint Board of Christian Education of Australia and New Zealand, 1984), 139.
3. Anderson and Hopkins, 145.
4. John H. Westerhoff III, *Living the Faith Community* (Minneapolis: Winston Press, 1985), 13.
5. Fred Kaan, "Help us accept each other," in *Songs for a Gospel People* (Winfield, B.C.: Wood Lake Books, 1987), #8.

Selected Bibliography

for further reading or study

On Spirituality

Anderson, S. R., and P. Hopkins. *The Feminine Face of God*. New York: Bantam Books, 1991. This book on women's spirituality is based on interviews with 200 women of a great variety of faith backgrounds. It helps everyone to understand the multiplicity of ways in which a spiritual life can be lived.

Berends, Polly Herrien. *Coming to Life: Traveling the Spiritual Path in Everyday Life*. San Francisco: Harper & Row, 1990. Easy to read and understand.

Furlong, Monica. *Contemplating Now*. Cambridge, Mass.: Cowley Publications, 1983. This book is about achieving balance in a busy life.

Gorsuch, John P. *An Invitation to the Spiritual Journey*. New York/Manwah: Paulist Press, 1990. Practical and Inspiring.

LeShan, Lawrence. *How to Meditate: A Guide to Self-Discovery*. Toronto: Bantam Books, 1974. Contains basic information about actual practice.

On Living in a Faith Community

Grierson, Denham. *Transforming a People of God*. Melbourne, Australia: The Joint Board of Christian Education of Australia and New Zealand, 1984. This book is based on experience and gives practical tools.

Hahn, Celia A. *Lay Voices in an Open Church*. Washington: The Alban Institute., 1985. This book is an excellent evaluative tool for churches working on a Mission Statement or trying to respond to Reginald Bibby's findings in *Unknown Gods* (Toronto: Stoddart Publishing, 1993).

Miller, Craig Kennet. *Baby Boomer Spirituality: Ten Essential Values of a Generation*. Nashville: Discipleship Resources, 1992. This book is a valuable guide to a significant part of every community.

Taylor, JoAnne. *Innocent Wisdom: Children as Spiritual Guides.* New York: The Pilgrim Press, 1984. An eye-opening book that helps us to affirm children as an important ingredient of a faith community.

Westerhoff, John H., III. *Living the Faith Community: The Church that Makes a Difference.* Oak Grove, Minn: Winston Press, 1985. This book helps one to see what a church could be like if all faithstyles were comfortable living together.

On Faith Development Theory and Practice

Burton, Laurel Arthur. *Pastoral Paradigms: Christian Ministry in a Pluralistic Culture.* Washington D.C.: The Alban Institute, 1988. A thought-provoking "systems" approach that recognizes our rapidly changing society.

Dykstra, Craig, and Sharon Parks, eds. *Faith Development and Fowler.* Birmingham, Ala.: Religious Education Press, 1986. A good way to get twelve points of view on the subject! Fowler does "A Dialogue Toward a Future."

Ford, Iris M. *Life Spirals: The Faith Journey.* Burlington: Welch Publishing Co. Inc., 1988. This book has a conversational style but a scholarly base.

Fowler, James W. *Stages of Faith: The Psychology of Human Development and the Quest for Meaning.* San Francisco: Harper & Row, 1981. Fowler's original research and conclusions.

———. *Faith Development and Pastoral Care.* Philadelphia: Fortress Press, 1987. Designed for pastors.

continued from page iv

Index